100

THINGS TO DO IN
ROCHESTER
BEFORE YOU
DIE

T0046615

Downtown Rochester
Photo courtesy Michael DeMaria

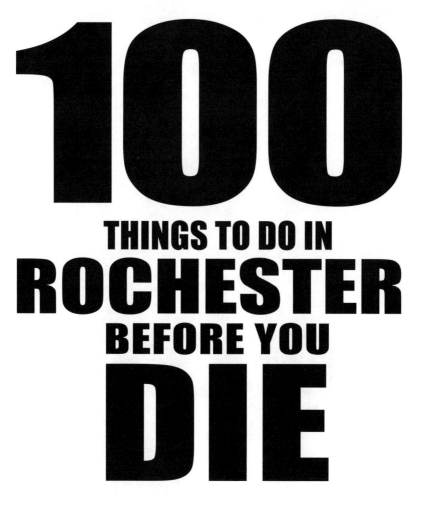

100
THINGS TO DO IN
ROCHESTER
BEFORE YOU
DIE

ROBIN L. FLANIGAN

REEDY PRESS

Library of Congress Control Number: 2022949258

ISBN: 9781681064284

Design by Jill Halpin

Cover photo by Michael DeMaria.
Author photo by Michelle Nicholson.

Printed in the United States of America
23 24 25 26 27   5 4 3 2

We (the publisher and the author) have done our best to provide the most accurate information available when this book was completed. However, we make no warranty, guarantee, or promise about the accuracy, completeness, or currency of the information provided, and we expressly disclaim all warranties, express or implied. Please note that attractions, company names, addresses, websites, and phone numbers are subject to change or closure, and this is outside of our control. We are not responsible for any loss, damage, injury, or inconvenience that may occur due to the use of this book. When exploring new destinations, please do your homework before you go. You are responsible for your own safety and health when using this book.

DEDICATION

To my dear friend Sue.
I had Kilimanjaro.
You had the Camino de Santiago.
We have Rochester.

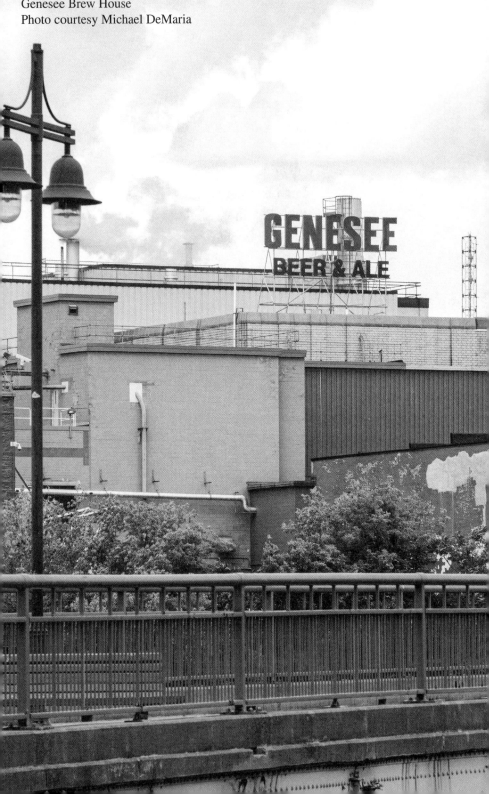

Genesee Brew House
Photo courtesy Michael DeMaria

CONTENTS

Music and Entertainment

● ●

Sports and Recreation

● ●

Culture and History

• •

Shopping and Fashion

• •

PREFACE

I've had a personal mantra for years: Know what you want. Work hard to get it. Accept what comes next.

When I was asked to write this book about Rochester, my adopted hometown, I knew immediately that I wanted to honor and celebrate the city in which I've spent nearly half my life. I moved here from North Carolina in 1999 to work as a beat reporter for the *Democrat and Chronicle* newspaper. My first winter I learned a valuable lesson: there is no bad weather, only inappropriate clothing. That's because Rochester is a vibrant, active place to be, even in the middle of a snowstorm.

In every season my journalism career—now focused on freelancing—exposes me to history, cultures, and experiences I may overlook without a notebook and pen in my hands. Over the past year I've taken this education and added to it countless hours of car trips, research, and revisions to transfer from my hands what now is in yours—an absolute labor of love.

As for the acceptance part, I only hope that what comes next is a lot of joy (and a fair share of surprise) as you use this book to delve deeper into what Rochester has to offer.

As New York State's fourth-largest city, Rochester has been nicknamed both Flour City and Flower City—nods to its past first as the country's largest producer of flour, then as home to the world's largest seed company. The municipal logo pays tribute to both identities by combining a flour-mill gear and a budding flower, a powerful statement about innovation and the universal truth that different things can be true at the same time.

What I know to be true is that Rochester is both big and small, both culturally sophisticated and quietly charming, both renowned the world over in some ways and a well-kept secret in others. And always endlessly fascinating.

Given the format of this book series, the following recommendations are by no means comprehensive, let alone exhaustive. They are, instead, an honest effort to salute a city that regularly earns national and international accolades for a reason.

A special thanks to all the friends, relatives, and strangers who offered suggestions and encouraging words. I couldn't have done this without you.

Oh, and one last thing. This book is mostly about places, but please notice the people. They're good ones.

Good Smoke
Photo courtesy Brian Wemett

FOOD AND DRINK

PUT CALORIES ON THE BACK BURNER
WITH A NICK TAHOU HOTS
GARBAGE PLATE

You're either devoted to or disgusted by Rochester's iconic junk food, which has earned ink in the *New York Times* (dubbing it "an outlaw dish") and inspired knockoffs around town. The Garbage Plate, trademarked by the landmark Nick Tahou Hots downtown, is a century-old, cheap, greasy mix of two sides (typically home fries and macaroni salad, but baked beans and french fries are other options) and a protein—two hamburgers or hot dogs. Jimmy Fallon once told Kevin Hart the dish would give him "spider powers." Often viewed as the ultimate hangover food, it packs a whopping 1,700 calories, weighs nearly three pounds, and once was named the fattiest food in New York State by health.com. Parking is behind the building.

320 W. Main St., 585-436-0184
www.garbageplate.com

HERE ARE SOME LOCAL VERSIONS OF THE GARBAGE PLATE

Mark's Texas Hots
"Sloppy Plate"
487 Monroe Ave., 585-473-1563
www.facebook.com/markstxhots

Empire Hots
"Trash Plate"
2209 Empire Blvd., Webster, 585-787-2110
www.empirehots.com

DogTown
"Junkyard Plate"
691 Monroe Ave., 585-271-6620
www.dogtownhots.com

The Red Fern
"Compost Plate" (vegan)
283 Oxford St., 585-563-7633
www.redfernrochester.com

BITE INTO A NEW TAKE ON A CLASSIC
AT SIMPLY CRÊPES

Sometimes a little spin goes a long way. Identifying as a progressively traditional French Canadian farmhouse kitchen, Simply Crêpes puts a creative twist on best-loved comfort foods. In 2019 that paid off when celebrity chef Fabio Viviani chose the restaurant's Rugby Crepe, based on the McDonald's Big Mac, to feature on the Food Network's *The Best Thing I Ever Ate*. (He called it "delicious, mischievous, and confusingly awesome.") Crêpes here are used just like bread or tortillas elsewhere—as a means to serve other food. Made-from-scratch dishes swing from sweet (lemon raspberry chiffon crepe) to savory (Thai curry crepe), with pure maple syrup as a key sweetener in sauces and dressings. Bonus: the Pittsford location is in a historic building opposite the Erie Canal.

7 Schoen Pl., Pittsford, 585-383-8310
1229 Bay Rd., Webster, 585-236-1056
101 S. Main St., Canandaigua, 585-394-9090
www.simplycrepes.com

SAVOR THE FLAVORS
AT ATLAS EATS KITCHEN & BAKE SHOP

Tucked into a residential neighborhood, Atlas Eats Kitchen & Bake Shop has developed a cult following for its rotating, internationally inspired menus. But the biggest buzz is about the eatery's Edible Atlas Dinner Series. Its five-course, $65-per-person tasting menu has one seating each Friday and Saturday night and often sells out. Selections change every two weeks and are posted online the weekend beforehand. All from-scratch recipes incorporate local produce and products, with the chef sometimes heading to specialty markets around the corner to ensure quality and authenticity. Don't come here for privacy. With only 24 indoor seats, the setting is intimate, though that's part of the charm.

2185 N. Clinton Ave., Irondequoit, 585-544-1300

www.atlas-eats.com

TOAST
TO A HISTORIC BEER
AT GENESEE BREW HOUSE

Want to help New York's oldest brewery decide whether to scale its next specialty line? Ruby Red Kolsch and Dry Hopped Cream Ale got their mass-produced start this way in the tasting room at the Genesee Brew House, which brings the storied Genesee Brewery to life. (The brewery was founded in 1878 and named for the Genesee River it overlooks; before refrigeration, the bedrock kept the beer cold.) You can't get any more classic here than the iconic Genesee Beer—affectionately nicknamed "Genny"—made with two-row barley malt, corn grits, and hops from Washington's Yakima Valley. Not an expensive brew by any means, but need to tighten the wallet even more? Genesee Cream Ale once led the list in a *Washington Post* Top-10 ranking of cheap beer.

25 Cataract St., 585-263-9200
www.geneseebeer.com

TIP

Drink or eat on Genesee Brew House's outdoor terrace or rooftop patio (Bavarian pretzels come with beer-flavored cheese sauce or beer-flavored mustard) for one of the best views of the city's High Falls waterfall.

ROCHESTER HAS A ROBUST CRAFT BEER SCENE. HERE ARE SOME DRAFT PICKS

Rohrbach Brewing Co.
97 Railroad St., 585-546-8020
3859 Buffalo Rd., 585-546-8020
www.rohrbachs.com

Three Heads Brewing
186 Atlantic Ave., 585-244-1224
www.threeheadsbrewing.com

Iron Tug Brewing
371 Park Ave., 585-738-5606
www.irontugbrewing.com

Swiftwater Brewing
378 Mt. Hope Ave., 585-530-3471
www.swiftwaterbrewing.com

Strangebird
62 Marshall St., 585-505-8700
www.strangebirdbeer.com

Fifth Frame Brewing Co.
155 St. Paul St., 585-735-7155
www.fifthframe.co

Sager Beer Works
46 Sager Dr., Suite E, 585-417-5404
www.sagerbeerworks.com

SOAK UP
THE BEACH SCENE
AT MARGE'S LAKESIDE INN

Marge's Lakeside Inn is a hidden gem along the Lake Ontario shoreline, an intoxicating backdrop for enjoying sunsets with a drink in your hand and toes in the sand. The site of an illicit speakeasy during Prohibition, the vintage watering hole—with an outdoor firepit, lounge area, and tiki bar—has transported patrons into instant vacation mode for more than six decades. Photos on the wood-paneled walls salute that history, as does an old-time jukebox (with handwritten labels) playing lots of Patsy Cline, Johnny Cash, and Elvis. Marge's can get crowded, especially when the weather cooperates, so if you prefer a more peaceful break from the real world, go early. The bar hosts live music outdoors most Wednesdays through Sundays.

4909 Culver Rd., 585-323-1020
www.margeslakesideinn.com

BUCKLE UP FOR A FLIGHT
AT LIVING ROOTS WINE & CO.

Compare and contrast your way through four 1.5-ounce wine servings at Living Roots Wine & Co., in the corner of a century-old industrial building. An artfully designed menu board details the character and process of each flight. The owners are a millennial, intercontinental couple. Colleen grew up in nearby Finger Lakes wine country; Sebastian is a sixth-generation winemaker from the Adelaide Hills region of South Australia. Midflight snack options include kangaroo jerky. The urban winery's organic aesthetic and small-batch wines have been featured in *Wine Spectator* and *Forbes*, while its 2019 Shale Creek Bone-Dry Riesling got props from *Wine Enthusiast* for offering "dense tones of tangerine, lemon oil, pine, and dry honeycomb on the nose." The winery's Finger Lakes wines are made on-site.

1255 University Ave., 585-383-1112
www.livingrootswine.com

FUN FACT

Glaciers at the end of the Ice Age are responsible for the sandy loam soil at Casa Larga Vineyards. As a result, the 45-acre estate is one of the best places in the Finger Lakes region to grow grapes (and is one of the region's oldest wineries). The two varietals grown here are European Vinifera and French-American hybrids.

2287 Turk Hill Rd., Fairport, 585-223-4210
www.casalarga.com

SAMPLE A MIX OF SPECIALTIES
AT ETHNIC BAKERIES

From Rochester's earliest days as a major manufacturing center, immigrants have enriched the city with their culinary contributions, and our palates are better for it. Bakeries are delectable places to broaden taste buds. At Voula's Greek Sweets, sample pourakia ("little cigars" in English), which are rolled baklava with toasted almonds, walnuts, and dried cranberries soaked in rosewater syrup and dipped in chocolate. Find cream cheese-filled quesitos, one of the most popular pastries in Puerto Rico, at Borinquen Bakery & Restaurant. Italian cookies at Savoia Pastry Shoppe are made using recipes handed down through three generations. Malek's Bakery, meanwhile, carries a decadent round babka with sumptuous chocolate swirls. Exercise portion control or your palate won't be the only thing expanding.

Voula's Greek Sweets
439 Monroe Ave., 585-242-0935
www.voulasgreeksweets.com

Savoia Pastry Shoppe
2267 Clifford Ave., 585-482-1130
www.savoiapastry.com

Borinquen Bakery & Restaurant
1195 N. Clinton Ave., 585-544-7455
www.facebook.com/
BorinquenBakery585

Malek's Bakery
1795 Monroe Ave., 585-461-1720
www.maleksbakery.com

TASTE A BIT OF POLAND
AT POLSKA CHATA

Polska Chata—meaning "old Polish house"—is an unassuming market, restaurant, and deli in a converted two-story house. Some customers are immigrants wanting groceries imported from their homeland. Some are descendants of immigrants wanting to connect with their heritage through food. (One who'd driven from Buffalo became emotional after eating the borscht.) And some simply are curious to learn about Polish cuisine. For a crash course, order the Polish Platter (also available vegan-style), a montage of delectable dishes starring stuffed cabbage topped with tomato sauce, bigos, kielbasa, pierogi, and mashed potatoes. A fair number of well-captioned photographs celebrate Polish history in Rochester dating back to the early 1900s. Think sauerkraut's just a topper? Owner Izabela Tarlowska suggests trying the sauerkraut soup.

32 Vinedale Ave., 585-266-4480
www.polskachata.us

TIP
If you want to bolster your self-worth when leaving Polska Chata, look at the sign above the door on your way out. In Polish, it translates to: "Our customers are the most expensive thing in our store."

CELEBRATE
(FOR ANY REASON)
AT GOOD LUCK

Once recognized by *Esquire* magazine as one of the best bars in America, Good Luck is a noisy nightspot for festive foodies who like family-style fare. Its number one seller by far is the one-pound Good Luck Burger—house-ground local beef on brioche with Cuba cheddar, vegetable slaw, and a massive mound of fries. All meat is super fresh, sourced locally, and butchered on-site. A square bar in the center of the restaurant doles out old-fashioned cocktails made with high-quality liquors and bitters (and using oversized ice cubes designed to melt exceptionally slowly). Sip a New York Sour while appreciating the open kitchen, exposed brick walls, and wooden beams. Reservations strongly recommended.

50 Anderson Ave., 585-340-6161
www.restaurantgoodluck.com

GO HOG WILD
AT GOOD SMOKE BBQ

The owners of Good Smoke BBQ weren't messing around from the get-go. They began the biz in 2006 to become competitive on the professional barbecue circuit. Six hundred national and international awards later—many from the esteemed Kansas City Barbeque Society—the East Rochester restaurant remains serious about its sauces. The OG BBQ sauce, heavy on molasses and cumin, is succulent on the pulled pork sandwich. Choose the Roc Style sauce for a sweeter tang. Bacon is another star: wrapped around meatballs ("Moink Balls"), crispy-fried and tossed in a rib glaze and pork rub ("Pig Candy"), or added to any entree for the price of a homemade side ($3.99). Indoors is no frills; if you can, eat on the inviting back patio beneath two huge hickory trees.

135 W. Commercial St., East Rochester, 585-203-1576
www.goodsmokebbq.com

TIP

Relish nationally acclaimed brisket and ribs at Dinosaur Bar-B-Que—located in a historic railway station, featured on various Food Network and Travel Channel shows, and once named the country's best barbecue joint on *Good Morning America*.

99 Court St, 585-325-7090
www.dinosaurbarbque.com/rochester

DELIGHT IN THE BAWDY PAST
AT RICHARDSON'S CANAL HOUSE

Richardson's Canal House may be on the National Register of Historic Places as the site of the oldest original Erie Canal inn. And it may serve upscale food with an Erie Canal view (and fair-weather canal-side dining). But make no mistake. There is more humor than hubris here, with servers offering informal, upon-request tours of the former brothel's upstairs rooms. As for the food, thick bordelaise sauce dresses the seven-ounce beef tenderloin, and pan-seared dry sea scallops melt in your mouth. Meals come with two kinds of house-made bread. After settling up, allow time to fully digest the hanky-panky in artist Edith Lunt Small's painting, "1825 Richardson's Tavern." One other fun fact? This used to be a nudist colony, too, in the 1930s.

1474 Marsh Rd., Pittsford, 585-248-5000
www.richardsonscanalhouse.com

ENJOY FARM-TO-MOUTH MILK
AT PITTSFORD FARMS DAIRY & BAKERY

Local farms provide the raw milk used at the quaint Pittsford Farms Dairy & Bakery, set in the historic village of Pittsford. Milk, chocolate milk, buttermilk, and eggnog are bottled on-site and sold in old-fashioned glass bottles. An in-house ice cream parlor serves up the cow juice in more than two dozen flavors year-round. That number soars in the summer, when lines routinely spill out the door. At least 50 flavors are sold in take-home quarts. (You won't be disappointed with Snapdragon, made with smooth, caramel-swirled vanilla ice cream and dusted with moist graham cracker crumbles.) Recommendation: grab a cone to go and enjoy while walking along the nearby Erie Canal.

44 N. Main St., Pittsford, 585-586-6610
www.pittsfordfarmsdairy.com

TREAT YOUR TASTE BUDS TO A CONE
AT ABBOTT'S FROZEN CUSTARD

Abbott's Frozen Custard is a diet staple in these parts. The creamy concoction is best enjoyed at the flagship stand on Lake Avenue, across the street from Ontario Beach Park. The stand has stood since 1926, when Arthur Abbott stopped traveling with small carnivals along the Eastern Seaboard to set up shop permanently. If you want to go old-school, try the slow-churned vanilla or chocolate (or both), with or without almonds. More adventurous? Order the signature frozen-on-a-stick Turtle made with custard, salty Spanish nuts, and gooey fudge. Abbott's is in the midst of a national expansion plan, with more than three dozen locations in seven states and more on the way. (But we'll always have the OG.)

4791 Lake Ave., 585-865-7400
www.abbottscustard.com

SWIRL AND SIP WHISKEY
AT BLACK BUTTON DISTILLING

Rochester's first grain-to-glass distillery since Prohibition, Black Button Distilling came in hot. In 2015, just three years after opening, it was one of *USA Today*'s 10 Best Craft Specialty Spirits Distilleries (then again in 2016 and 2017). And the awards have kept coming. Ask for a smooth Four Grain Straight Bourbon Whiskey—warm baking spices, classic caramel, and vanilla, with a lingering spice-and-oak finish. A head-to-head rival with Kentucky's finest, Black Button makes "Rochester Style" bourbon the way no one in the Bluegrass State can, with limestone-filtered regional lake water, grain from nutrient-rich Finger Lakes soil, oak barrels stored in fluctuant Northeastern temperatures, and other ingredients grown or produced in New York State. Cheers to that.

1344 University Ave., 585-730-4512
www.blackbuttondistilling.com

INDULGE IN
THE BEST OF THE SEASON
AT A HURD ORCHARDS LUNCHEON

The setting for a Hurd Orchards farm-to-table luncheon would make Martha Stewart jealous. The flower-filled, 200-year-old English threshing barn with hand-hewn beams alone is magazine-worthy. Menus are based on family recipes, peak seasonal crops, and edible flowers grown on the farm, some parts of which have been in the family since the early 1800s. Zesty zinnias pair nicely with zucchini tarts. Spring greens featuring apricots, donut peaches, blackberries, raspberries, cherry tomatoes, and cucumbers get tossed with peach buttermilk dressing. Amy and her mom Sue, who co-own the farm, give an enthusiastic history of the grounds to welcome guests. Pricey but worth every penny, luncheons include a salad, main plate, bread plate, dessert, and beverage. Reservations required, prepaid, nontransferrable, and nonrefundable.

17260 Ridge Rd., Holley, 585-638-8838
www.hurdorchards.com

TIP

The adjoining Hurd Orchards market is equally quaint. Ogle over hand-embroidered tea towels and just-baked breads. If you want to make your own goodies with the orchard's bounty, dress down and come during pick-your-own hours during any fruit-bearing season.

RELAX WITH ONE OF THE WORLD'S FINEST BREWS
AT HAPPY EARTH TEA

Nicknamed the "champagne of teas," Darjeeling comes from a mountainous region in West Bengal, India, where Happy Earth Tea co-owner Niraj Lama was born, raised, and began his business. Lama returns there regularly to work directly with certified organic tea gardens, a contributing factor in Happy Earth Tea being one of only six tea purveyors recommended by food magazine *Bon Appétit* in April 2022. A first-flush spring Darjeeling yields notes of peach, sweet grass, and green mangoes. Pull up a chair at the bar to hear Lama softly wax poetic about this delicate black tea served in glass mugs because "the color is a big part of the enjoyment." The shop offers 60 certified organic loose-leaf teas from around the world, steeped using western or traditional methods.

696 South Ave., 585-730-7754
www.happyearthtea.com

DEVOUR A HOT DOG
ROCHESTER-STYLE

Coney Island has nothing on Rochester's "white hot." This regional favorite is a combination of pork, beef, and veal—each uncured and unsmoked, giving the hot dog a white hue. Look for the brand Zweigle's—Rochester-based butchers since 1880— at Bill Gray's, SeaBreeze Lakeview Hots, and other regional chain mainstays. DogTown, which tosses 18 unique varieties of toppings atop hot dogs nestled in French bread, can replace any regular dog with a white hot upon request. If you're downtown, order from a food cart. (Look for the red-and-yellow umbrellas.) If you want to eat the pop-open frankfurter like a local, top it with meat hot sauce, mustard, and chopped onion.

Bill Gray's
4870 Culver Rd., 585-266-7820
www.billgrays.com

SeaBreeze Lakeview Hots
4671 Culver Rd., 585-222-4687
www.seabreezelakeviewhots.com

DogTown
691 Monroe Ave., 585-271-6620
www.dogtownhots.com

BITE INTO A JUICY ONE
AT SCHUTT'S APPLE MILL

Oh, so many ways to partake of the forbidden fruit at Schutt's Apple Mill. Homemade apple cider fried cakes and sundaes. Apples at the peck stand, with more than 30 varieties once fall rolls around. Apple Frost, the mill's own melt-on-your-tongue mixture of soft-serve vanilla ice cream and sweet cider. And free cider samples. Schutt's has been in the same family since 1918, which is why its hard cider is named Great Grandpa's Grog, after founder Paul Schutt. Sample some of it in the tasting room, held up with barnwood walls once belonging to the family's original barn across the street. Now owned by fifth-generation farmer and fourth-generation shop owner Evan Schutt, the mill, unlike most farm stands, is open year-round.

1063 Plank Rd., Webster, 585-872-2924
www.schuttsapplemill.com

TIP

Pick your own apples in the Schutt's Apple Mill orchard across the road—starting in late August with Sweet Maias and Premier Honeycrisps and going through late October with Fujis and EverCrisps.

SHARE IN A HOLIDAY TRADITION
WITH SPECIAL TOUCH BAKERY

It's all about the pies. Ten thousand of them at Thanksgiving time. What started 30-plus years ago as a vocational training opportunity for people with intellectual and developmental disabilities has turned into a full-fledged business with a national following. In 2017, Special Touch Bakery expanded from a 700-square-foot school kitchen to a 20,000-square-foot state-of-the-art commercial bakery. The nonprofit provides meaningful employment for people of all abilities and produces 15,000 all-natural, made-from-scratch pies a week. Its specialties: gourmet fruit, natural juice, dessert, cream, and sugar-free varieties. The by-far crowd favorite is the apple crumb loaded with sliced apples and mixed with cinnamon.

Aman's Farm & Market
2458 E. Ridge Rd., Irondequoit,
585-544-8360
www.facebook.com/
AmansFarmMarket

The Village Fair
119 W. Commercial St.,
East Rochester, 585-586-1637
www.facebook.com/
eastrochestervillagefair

Red Bird Market
130 Fairport Village Landing,
Fairport, 585-377-5050
www.facebook.com/redbirdmarket

Dell's Market & Deli
1799 English Rd., 585-368-0840
www.dellsmarket.com

TUCK INTO A REGIONAL CULINARY INVENTION
AT GRANDPA SAM'S ITALIAN KITCHEN

When the *New York Times* named Chicken French its most popular recipe in 2018, Rochesterians were proud as peacocks. We take credit for the Italian-American dish, served with a lemon-wine sauce and a ubiquitous option around town. That's because a chef here in the 1970s seems to have been the first to substitute sautéed chicken cutlets for then-standard veal. If you want a different take on the recipe, head to Grandpa Sam's Italian Kitchen in Spencerport, where the chicken is thin and tender and the sauce thicker than usual. (In 2016 the restaurant made travel website OnlyInYourState's "The 12 Places You Should Eat in New York" list.) Fans can take home a 24-ounce jar of Grandpa Sam's French Sauce for $6.99.

138 S. Union St., Spencerport, 585-349-7267
www.grandpasamsitaliankitchen.com

Eastman Theatre
Photo courtesy Michael DeMaria

MUSIC
AND ENTERTAINMENT

PLAY AT THE WORLD'S LARGEST TOY MUSEUM
AT THE STRONG
NATIONAL MUSEUM OF PLAY

The sights . . . the sounds . . . the senses won't know what hit them. What in the late '60s was the "Margaret Woodbury Strong Museum of Fascination" has become the Strong National Museum of Play—a highly interactive maze of amusements amid the world's largest collection of toys, dolls, board games, and electronic games. Sit on a replica of the Sesame Street stoop. Debate whether the rubber duck belongs in the museum's National Toy Hall of Fame. (It was inducted in 2013.) Follow a yellow brick road to five magical worlds inspired by children's literature. A 90,000-square-foot expansion, expected to open in summer 2023, will examine technology and play, and be home to the World Video Game Hall of Fame. A great place for kids to explore and adults to reminisce.

1 Manhattan Square, 585-263-2700
www.museumofplay.org

TIP
Leave plenty of time—and add $5 to your admission fee—to walk among hundreds of free-flying butterflies in the museum's Dancing Wings Butterfly Garden.

GROOVE
TO GARTH FAGAN DANCE

Witnessing the work of internationally acclaimed dance choreographer Garth Fagan, who has made Rochester home for more than 50 years, is a visual feast. Jamaican-born Fagan, the choreographer behind Broadway's *The Lion King*, has earned a Tony Award, a Laurence Olivier Award, and other notable recognition for his distinctive technique, which combines the sense of weight in modern dance, the speed and precision of ballet, the torso-centered movements and energy of Afro-Caribbean rhythms, and the rule-breaking tenets of postmodern dance. Dynamic and original, emotional and abstract, Fagan's dancers display awe-inspiring stamina as they leap, spiral, and otherwise transport their elastic bodies across the stage. Fagan's studio is the only place worldwide that teaches the Fagan technique. (Classes are open for children, teens, and adults.)

50 Chestnut St., 585-454-3260
www.garthfagandance.org

KICK OFF
FESTIVAL SEASON
AT THE ROCHESTER LILAC FESTIVAL

If ever there was a time to stop and smell the flowers, this is it. Each May, the Rochester Lilac Festival in Highland Park draws visitors from around the globe to admire nearly 600 varieties of the fragrant shrub—the largest collection in the United States. (Doing its part to promote the "Flower City.") A single floret of the rare "Rochester" lilac strain, bred by one of the park's former horticulturists, may spawn up to 25 petals. Not a landscape lover? Many flock to the fest for live music, arts-and-crafts shows, children's entertainment, and other events. Lilac blooms are weather-dependent but not to worry—the park's 35 varieties of magnolias and other floral collections are worthy in their own right.

Highland Park
180 Reservoir Ave.
www.rochesterevents.com/lilac-festival

OTHER WELL-KNOWN FESTIVALS AROUND ROCHESTER

Rochester International Jazz Festival
www.RochesterJazz.com

Rochester Fringe Festival
www.rochesterfringe.com

Fairport Canal Days
www.fairportcanaldays.com

Corn Hill Arts Festival
www.cornhillartsfestival.com

M&T Bank Clothesline Festival
www.mag.rochester.edu/events/clothesline-festival

Annunciation Rochester Greek Festival
www.rochestergreekfestival.com

WATCH
HIGHLY FLAMMABLE FILM
AT THE DRYDEN THEATRE

From a twisty noir one night to a neorealistic classic the next, the Nitrate Picture Show pays tribute each June to a type of film so flammable it burns underwater. (Kodak discontinued its use in 1952). The world's first festival of film conservation is held at the Dryden Theatre, one of only five theaters in the country and a handful in the world certified to project the combustible 35mm prints. The visual aesthetic of these motion pictures—one showing dated back to 1913—is shimmering and luminous. A heavy gold curtain, slowly rising before each screening, is another theatrical throwback. Learn more at a lecture or workshop on the art and science of film preservation. As a tease, the official program is kept secret until the festival's first day.

900 East Ave., 585-327-4800
www.eastman.org/dryden-theatre

TIP

Quick history lesson: the Dryden Theatre is attached to the George Eastman Museum and named after George Dryden, widower of George Eastman's niece, Ellen. The venue hosts cinema's most talented directors, cinematographers, actors, animators, critics, and other film industry faves.

GO FOR A SPIN
ON THE ONTARIO BEACH CAROUSEL

Have you ridden a horse on a merry-go-round? Yawn. The Dentzel Menagerie Carousel has 52 hand-carved animals of different species to choose from. Not only that, its location at Ontario Beach Park means you catch a lake view as you're circling around—on a lion, a mule, an ostrich?—for nearly four minutes. Music bellows from an old Stinson Band organ in the corner (sometimes live, sometimes recorded). Built by the G.A. Dentzel Co. of Philadelphia in 1905, it is one of the oldest continuously operating carousels in the country and one of only a few remaining Dentzel carousels still spinning. $1 a ride; $5 buys a ride-all-day wristband. Typically open Memorial Day through Labor Day weekends.

4800 Lake Ave.
www.cityofrochester.gov/article.aspx?id=8589938342

TIP

In 2016, community activists were successful in getting a carousel panel that included a derogatory portrayal of Black children replaced with an image of a black panther, a symbol of power in the Black community. That panel is part of the Take It Down! Organizing against Racism permanent exhibit at RMSC, the museum and science center.

TAKE A MUSICAL JOURNEY
WITH THE ROCHESTER
PHILHARMONIC ORCHESTRA

A year after motion-picture film pioneer George Eastman built the magnificent, Italian Renaissance–style Eastman Theatre (now called Kodak Hall at Eastman Theatre) in 1922, he formed the Rochester Philharmonic Orchestra to put music to the day's black-and-white films. The orchestra's Pops Series continues to marry music and film by pairing live scores with big-screen blockbusters. (Harry Potter movies are a favorite.) Although classical compositions are the cornerstone of the orchestra, which has played Carnegie Hall, performances are more progressive than stodgy, often blending genres at more than 150 events each season—many at no charge. Family-friendly concerts sometimes include free pre-performance activities for younger concertgoers. In summertime, orchestra musicians play free concerts at parks and other outdoor spaces around the region.

255 East Ave., 585-454-2100
www.rpo.org

JIVE AND JAM
AT THE ROCHESTER INTERNATIONAL JAZZ FESTIVAL

One the world's largest jazz festivals, Rochester International Jazz Festival is nine days of top-notch melody, harmony, rhythm, and improvisation. Travel site Culture Trip called it the world's best jazz festival in 2019. Bop between 20 venues to take in the sounds of more than 1,750 artists—rising stars to legendary musicians—from countries near and far, all putting their spin on the American art form. Festival favorite Trombone Shorty once drew 40,000 people. New musical discoveries await around every corner. Producers Marc Iacona and John Nugent are always saying, "It's not just who you know, it's who you don't know." Outdoor shows and jazz workshops with visiting artists are free. Club passes for the June event are good at all 12 club venues, but not Kodak Hall.

585-454-2060
www.rochesterjazz.com

TIP

The party isn't over when the last band unplugs. Jam sessions start at 10:30 p.m. nightly at the Hyatt Regency Rochester downtown—and you never know who will show up to play. Past pop-ins include Wynton Marsalis, Jake Shimabukuro, and Robin Thicke's band members. No cover charge.

SATISFY YOUR INNER CINEPHILE
AT THE LITTLE THEATRE

The art deco-style Little Theatre opened in 1929 as a silent picture house during the last year of the silent film era. To survive it had to pivot fast, but its new focus on experimental talking pictures worked, and now the Little is the oldest continuously running independent film theater in the country. This is Rochester's hub for indie and foreign films. If you want more meaning out of your cinematic experience, catch movies paired with occasional postscreening panel discussions on race, gender, domestic violence, and other socially relevant topics. The monthly High Falls Women in Film Series promotes work by women behind and in front of the lens. Grab a bite or drink before or after a show at the Little Café.

240 East Ave., 585-258-0400
www.thelittle.org

THE LITTLE THEATRE HOSTS FILM FESTIVALS ANNUALLY. HERE ARE TWO.

ImageOut:
The Rochester LGBT Film & Video Festival
A highlight of the festival, going since 1993,
is Archival Night, featuring queer classics from
George Eastman House Motion Picture Archives
and other film archives.
www.imageout.org/index.php

Rochester Teen Film Festival
This collaborative, juried media competition honors
urban, suburban, and rural teen filmmakers (ages
13–18) in the Rochester region.
www.wxxi.org/teenfilmfestival#RTFF

PRACTICE YOUR PUTT
AT PARKSIDE WHISPERING PINES

Miniature golf courses these days are like miniature theme parks, with castles and forts and dinosaurs. Parkside Whispering Pines doesn't need that sort of schtick. As the country's oldest operating mini-golf course, it has one thing those other places could never have, and that's nostalgia. The cramped, 18-hole course definitely has a homespun feel, starting with payment at a small white shack next to the Parkside Diner. Maneuver around winding obstacles and elevation changes at stops named after popular local haunts and locales. A hole-in-one at the last hole (named, suitably, Parkside) wins you a free game. Children 5 and under are free. First game is $9; second game is $3.

4383 Culver Rd., Irondequoit, 585-323-1570
www.parksidediner.com

NOTE THE TALENT
AT AN EASTMAN SCHOOL
OF MUSIC PERFORMANCE

At the esteemed Eastman School of Music, some of the world's most accomplished student musicians perform more than 800 concerts each year—and almost all of them are free. Be exposed to every kind of music, from large orchestra, wind ensemble, jazz, and choral ensembles to chamber music, contemporary music (including new works by student composers), and solo piano and organ recitals. Most concerts draw a student-heavy crowd, so the mood tends to be informal and enthusiastic. Take equal heed of the venues. Intimate Kilbourn Hall is considered one of the finest chamber music halls in existence. Hatch Recital Hall is modern, with state-of-the-art acoustical and multimedia technology. And Kodak Hall at Eastman Theatre is splendorous, with a chandelier containing 20,000 pieces of European crystal.

26 Gibbs St., 585-274-1000
www.esm.rochester.edu

TIP

Even if you have no need to walk from Kodak Hall at Eastman Theatre to Hatch Hall (or vice versa), do it anyway. The space in between is Wolk Atrium, home to a striking blue-and-gold, light-reflecting chandelier by renowned glass artist Dale Chihuly.

CATCH A RISING STAR
AT GEVA THEATRE

What do Robert Downey Jr. and Josh Brolin have in common aside from *The Avengers*? They both performed as emerging actors on the stage at Geva Theatre, known for giving up-and-coming theater artists and innovative playwrights space to develop their work. As a result, audiences often get first crack at world premieres. The stage has helped foster 35 world premieres over the past 30 years—one of which, Gabriel Jason Dean's *Heartland*, made its off-Broadway debut in 2022. Among the stage's notable alumni: four Academy Award nominees, 22 Tony Award winners, and 11 Emmy Award winners. The past is as interesting as the future at Geva, which used to be a convention hall (it hosted President Theodore Roosevelt) and, later, a hospital during the 1918 flu epidemic.

75 Woodbury Blvd., 585-232-4382
www.gevatheatre.org

TIP

Geva former artistic director Mark Cuddy's adaption of *A Christmas Carol*, the Charles Dickens classic, has been a Rochester tradition since 1985. It is one of the theater's most popular productions and runs from late November to late December.

TRY SOMETHING NEW
AT ROCHESTER BRAINERY

Learn stuff: how to identify trees, unleash negativity, balance flavors to make the perfect cocktail. Make stuff: woodblock carvings, tortillas and arepas, pigments from flower petals. No subject seems unworthy at Rochester Brainery, a community classroom of sorts that brings together local businesses and people who like to try new things. (Those wanting to forge metal into a rose, for instance, meet at Rochester Arc + Flame Center.) Workshops often sell out because they're single session only so don't require a big time commitment—and you might walk away with a stained glass bird. Makes a great date night.

585-730-7034
www.rochesterbrainery.com

MEDITATE TO MUSIC FROM ACROSS THE AGES
AT COMPLINE

Contemplative. Ethereal. The sacred music performed by the Christ Church Schola Cantorum pays homage to Compline, the fourth-century monastic custom of private prayer and devotion before bedtime. For 30 minutes, listeners in candlelit pews are treated to Gregorian chant, Renaissance and baroque choral music, and choral improvisation by an acclaimed vocal ensemble at downtown's Gothic Revival-style Christ Church Rochester. Compline is at 9 p.m. on Sunday nights from October through April to accommodate the academic calendar, since many of the musicians are Eastman School of Music students. An ancient practice that has withstood the test of time, this is a modern musical meditation like no other. Admission is free; donations are appreciated.

141 East Ave., 585-454-3878
www.christchurchrochester.org/index.php/compline-2

TIP

A candlelight concert starts at
8:30 p.m. on the first Sunday of the month
during the Compline season. Some feature
Eastman School of Music's Craighead-
Saunders organ, a process reconstruction of a
late baroque instrument from 1776 and unlike
any other contemporary organ in existence.
All other Sundays during the season
include a 10-minute organ prelude.

TRAVEL THROUGH SPACE AND TIME
AT THE RMSC STRASENBURGH PLANETARIUM

Here's your ticket to any place in the known universe. Using the latest data from NASA and the world's observatories, the RMSC Strasenburgh Planetarium's state-of-the-art projection system extends a front-row seat to constellations, planets, recently discovered exoplanets, moons, black holes, and other parts of the final frontier. The new Digistar 7 full-dome projection system creates an immersive environment, though the original, all-analog 1968 Carl Zeiss Mark VI star projector still makes a monthly appearance for "Stars with Carl" shows. Laser light shows are set to music on most Saturdays (Dave Matthews, Led Zeppelin) and during the holiday season (Mariah Carey to Mannheim Steamroller). The planetarium building itself was designed to resemble a spiral nebula—a coiling galaxy just like the Milky Way. Far out.

657 East Ave., 585-697-1945
www.rmsc.org/strasenburghplanetarium

TIP

A once-top-secret spy satellite camera, built by Kodak in 1967, sits in the planetarium lobby. The GAMBIT system—an ancestor to the Hubble Space Telescope—helped prevent a potential World War III by spotting Soviet missile bases from space.

PARTY IN THE PARK
AT PARTY IN THE PARK

Talk about summertime savings. From June through August, on most Thursday nights, catch two opening bands and a leading act for under $10 at the Party in the Park Concert Series. Hear blues, funk, rock, reggae, and classic rock from national names, popular tribute bands, and regional musical talent. Past performers include Rochester native Lou Gramm of Foreigner fame, Lucinda Williams, George Clinton and Parliament Funkadelic, and X Ambassadors. Children 12 and under are free. (With the savings, you can always go VIP and get complimentary chair massages, climate-controlled restrooms, and more.) Gates open at 5 p.m., a half hour before the first performance. Plenty of portable bathrooms, helpful after hitting up the food trucks and craft beer vendors.

Dr. Martin Luther King Jr. Memorial Park
353 Court St.
www.rochesterevents.com

EXHIBIT YOUR WILD SIDE
AT SENECA PARK ZOO

More than 90 animal species live in five ecosystems at Seneca Park Zoo, named for its placement inside Frederick Law Olmsted-designed Seneca Park. The 20-acre zoo is one of the country's top breeders of African penguins among those accredited by the Association of Zoos and Aquariums. In warmer weather, the best time for seeing most animals in action is in the morning or toward day's end. Anytime is good in winter for snow leopards, polar bears, and red pandas, who love being active when temps drop. Get close to lions in a replica of Tanzania's Ngorongoro Crater. Feed a giraffe some lettuce for $5 (tickets often sell out). Tired of walking? Jump on a tram ($2 adults; $1 kids). Three overflow parking lots accommodate the most crowded days.

2222 St. Paul St., 585-336-7200
www.senecaparkzoo.org

TIP

Drink beer, save elephants at Seneca Park Zoo's ZooBrew. A portion of each ticket to monthly after-hours mixers in summer (with live music, beer, wine, and food) goes to conservation efforts. Say hello to the zoo's three elephants—Genny C, Lilac, and Moki. They understand more than 50 verbal commands and are the only African elephants in New York.

www.senecaparkzoo.org/zoobrew

CHILL OUT TO BELLS
AT THE HOPEMAN CARILLON
SUMMER CONCERT SERIES

A rare breed of instrument with roots in the 16th century hangs in the tower of the University of Rochester's Rush Rhees Library. One of only seven carillons in New York State, the more-than-three-ton Hopeman Memorial Carillon is played with fists, fingers, and feet and has 50 bells—all with a minor-third overtone. (This overtone is the signature sound of a properly tuned bell.) On Wednesday evenings in July, bring a chair or blanket to the University's Eastman Quadrangle, lined with red oaks, to hear national and international artists perform. Afterward, carilloneurs make their way down from the tower to chat (allow about 10 minutes for them to exit). The free, hour-long concerts start at 6:30 p.m. and happen rain or shine.

www.facebook.com/HopemanCarillon

TIP

The Hopeman Carillon Summer Concert Series has free parking available after 4 p.m. in the University of Rochester's Library Lot. University student carilloneurs play on most Sunday afternoons during the academic year (free parking in the Library Lot on weekends).

PREPARE TO BE HAUNTED
BY THE LADY IN WHITE
ON A GHOST WALK

The Lady in White has haunted Rochesterians for generations. Since the late 1800s, sightings have been recorded of a grieving mother searching for her missing daughter. Visit the scenes of those sightings with Rochester Candlelight Ghost Walks tour guide Jenni Lynn. Dressed as the infamous ghostess, she leads nighttime tours past Seabreeze Amusement Park, Union Tavern, and other lakeside attractions affiliated with the tale. Use ghost-hunting equipment while hearing the history of those places—the Union Tavern sits on the old foundation of a home built by a rumored pirate—interwoven with Lady in White legend lore. Parental discretion is advised for the hour-long tours, held rain or shine (so dress accordingly) on Saturdays in October.

585-542-8687
www.rochesterghosts.com

TIP
The tour doesn't go to the White Lady's Castle—a medieval-looking ruin at the eastern edge of Durand-Eastman Park on Lakeshore Boulevard, across from Lake Ontario. If you dare to drop by on your own, see if the ghost awaits at the top of the sinister staircase.

CHOOSE
YOUR FAVORITE FLAVOR
AT THE JELL-O GALLERY MUSEUM

Colorful, jiggly Jell-O shot to fame with a marketing campaign touting it as "America's Most Famous Dessert." That was in 1904, seven years after the moldable substance debuted in strawberry, raspberry, lemon, and orange flavors. The Jell-O Gallery Museum, relatively small but worth the 30-minute drive from Rochester, chronicles the advertising and marketing of this iconic American product. View hundreds of molds and all kinds of memorabilia—including baseball trading cards, a Jell-O-themed Barbie doll, and a huge Jell-O-themed arch from the 2004 Salt Lake City Olympics. Staff members offer brief sit-down history lessons upon arrival and encourage voting for your favorite flavor; there are 22 now. Perhaps plan your visit on July 12, otherwise known as National Eat Your Jell-O Day.

23 E. Main St., Le Roy, 585-768-7433
www.jellogallery.org

TIP

Head downstairs for another kind of archival experience—a transportation exhibition, including a reproduction Jell-O wagon, maintained by the LeRoy Historical Society. And as long as you're making the drive, check out the adjacent Historic LeRoy House, a 19th-century mansion-turned-museum.

EMBRACE THE MAGIC OF WINTER
AT ROC HOLIDAY VILLAGE

Rochesterians are a hearty bunch, so we can handle an outdoor festival in the freezing, snowy month of December. Held for at least 14 days, Roc Holiday Village (Roc, as locals know, is short for Rochester) turns downtown's Dr. Martin Luther King Jr. Memorial Park into a magical wonderland. Some have compared it to being in a Hallmark movie. The best part aside from heated tents? Almost everything is free: admission, ice skating, crafts, entertainment, even visits and photos with Santa. (Sign up with the Santa Text Express for an alert when your wait is down to five minutes.) Bring money for food, drinks, and handcrafted gifts. Or rent a cozy igloo for 90 minutes. Around 100,000 people each year enjoy this enchanting event.

353 Court St.
www.rocholidayvillage.com

TIP

While ice skating is free, the number of rental skates is limited; if you have a pair, bring them. Paid parking is available at surface lots and ramp garages nearby.

High Falls
Photo courtesy Michael DeMaria

SPORTS
AND RECREATION

COMMUNE WITH NATURE
AT WASHINGTON GROVE

Surprise! On the southeastern side of the city sits a 26-acre old-growth forest, home to red, white, and black oak trees dating back centuries. It's easy to forget you're in the city when you walk Washington Grove's moderately challenging 1.6-mile loop trail, past urban wildlife and more than 110 native plant species. The wooded sanctuary also is a major feeding and nesting area for birds (pileated woodpecker sightings are common), especially during spring and fall migration. Named after George Washington, it's on the eastern edge of Cobbs Hill Reservoir—a destination in itself with one of the best views of downtown Rochester. Dedicated parkland since 1912, Washington Grove was inducted into the Old-Growth Forest Network in 2021, to be protected forever from development. and logging.

TIP

The easiest-to-find Washington Grove trailhead is at the dead end of Nunda Boulevard, off Winton Road.

RIDE THE RABBIT
AT SEABREEZE AMUSEMENT PARK

You get a scream with a view from the top of the wooden Jack Rabbit—one of the oldest continuously operating roller coasters in the country. That's because historic Seabreeze Amusement Park is situated at the picturesque corner of Lake Ontario and Irondequoit Bay. With 60 attractions inside a manageable footprint, Seabreeze is no Six Flags theme park, which is part of its charm (as is the hand-carved carousel). In fact, wholesome family fun is one reason Seabreeze came in at #15 on TripAdvisor's 2021 list of the nation's best theme parks. Bring a bathing suit for dodging four-foot waves or plunging four stories down a dark tunnel at the adjoining water park (included with admission). High-flying acrobatic shows daily. Perk alert: parking is free.

4600 Culver Rd., 585-323-1900
www.seabreeze.com

Seabreeze Amusement Park
Photo courtesy Seabreeze Amusement Park

ROLL WITH IT
AT RADIO SOCIAL

More social club than bowling alley, Radio Social brings an upscale, midcentury touch to tenpins. No bolted-down plastic chairs here. Instead, 1960s lounge-style seating and coffee tables dot 34 bowling lanes—eight lanes in the front cocktail bar, 26 in the back whiskey bar. But that's only part of the lure of this former warehouse, a one-time producer of Stromberg-Carlson radios (hence the name) during World War II. Food options are a marriage of bowling alley classics (think brick-oven pizzas) and contemporary takes on Middle Eastern fare nodding to the owner's Israeli heritage. Strike a pose in front of the mustard-yellow couch and six shelves of vintage radios by the front door. Lanes start at $30 an hour.

20 Carlson Rd., 585-244-1484
www.radio-social.com

BEHOLD THE POWER OF AN URBAN WATERFALL
AT HIGH FALLS

A 96-foot waterfall smack in the middle of downtown helped spur Rochester's industrial development and, as our own miniature Niagara Falls, stands as one of the most impressive waterfalls in New York State. Walk along the 858-foot-long Pont de Rennes Bridge for the best view of High Falls, a Genesee River gorge more than 20,000 years in the making—and take in the downtown skyscape while you're at it. A self-guided walking tour of the Brown's Race Historic District, a collection of 19th-century buildings, tells the story of Rochester's rich milling, manufacturing, and tool-making history. Find an original millstone from the Moseley and Motley Milling Company, flour producers here from the 1850s to the mid-1920s.

TIP

Know your professional waterfall jumper history. After two death-defying leaps over Niagara Falls, Sam Patch, renowned nationally as America's first daredevil, set his sights on Rochester's High Falls in 1829. A crowd of thousands watched Patch—and his pet bear—jump successfully. Disappointed with the turnout, Patch planned a second attempt, prophetically marketed as "Sam's Last Jump" (intended to refer to his final plunge of the season). Thousands showed up again, only to be shocked when Patch hit the water with an audible thwack and disappeared. His body resurfaced months later.

TAKE YOURSELF OUT TO THE BALL GAME
AT INNOVATIVE FIELD

On the baseball field since 1877, the Rochester Red Wings is the oldest minor-league team in the history of professional sports. The Triple-A affiliate of the Washington Nationals called Cal Ripken one of their own before his Hall of Fame career with the Baltimore Orioles. "Let's have some fun!" is how General Manager Dan Mason starts every game, and that's because a lot of the entertainment that happens here takes place off the field. Just some of the promotions: Thursday is College Night, with a pregame happy hour. Postgame fireworks are on Friday and Saturday nights from late May through the end of the season. Every Sunday, kids can run the bases with mascots Spikes and Mittsy. Go on Tuesdays for two-for-one tickets.

1 Morrie Silver Way, 585-454-1001
www.milb.com/rochester

OTHER PROFESSIONAL SPORTS TEAMS IN ROCHESTER

Rochester Americans (Amerks)
Professional ice hockey team in the American Hockey League; owned and operated affiliate of the Buffalo Sabres.
www.amerks.com

Rochester Knighthawks
Professional box lacrosse team in the National Lacrosse League.
www.rochesterknighthawks.com

Rochester New York FC
American professional soccer team.
www.rnyfc.com

MAKE FEATHERED FRIENDS
AT THE WILD WINGS BIRD SANCTUARY

Eagles, owls, and a peregrine falcon—the fastest creature on earth—are just some of the permanently injured birds in lifelong residence at raptor refuge Wild Wings. Unable to survive on their own in the wild, more than 25 birds of prey are given sanctuary here, at the edge of Mendon Ponds Park. Most seem genuinely curious about their visitors, which makes it easy—and fun—to engage in staring contests. Learn about each species (American kestrels, for instance, will lose half their population by 2075 if current logging trends continue) from knowledgeable volunteers and signs. Admission is free, but because Wild Wings receives no private or county funding, do a solid and donate at the door.

27 Pond Rd., Mendon, 585-334-7790
www.wildwingsinc.com

TIP

Rehabilitated amphibians, reptiles, and mammals live permanently at the adjoining Wild Wings Nature Center. Say hello to two smoothie-loving opossum sisters abandoned when their mother got hit by a car, and a plucky porcupine who shattered a hind limb after falling out of a tree.

EXPLORE THE "EMERALD NECKLACE" OF PARKS

Rochester is one of only four cities nationwide with a park system designed by Frederick Law Olmsted, the father of American landscape architecture and innovative draftsman behind Manhattan's Central Park. Olmsted's 19th-century designs showcase the city's waterways as an "emerald necklace" of parks and gardens along the Genesee River, from the Erie Canal to Lake Ontario. Picnic near the reservoir set in the glacial terrain and botanical splendor of Highland Park. Access a statewide network of bicycle trails in Genesee Valley Park, where three gracefully arched bridges span calm waters. Hike down to the undisturbed shoreline of the Genesee at Seneca Park to see red-winged blackbirds among the reeds of river grass. And snap pictures of more than 250 cultivars in a nationally accredited rose garden at Maplewood Park.

Highland Park
Reservoir Ave.
www.monroecounty.gov/
parks-highland

Seneca Park
2222 St. Paul St.
www.monroecounty.gov/
parks-seneca

Genesee Valley Park
1000 E. River Rd.
www.cityofrochester.gov/
geneseevalleypark

Maplewood Park
Maplewood Dr. and Seneca Prkwy.
www.cityofrochester.gov/
maplewoodpark

POSE ON A PADDLEBOARD
AT BAYCREEK PADDLING CENTER

Picture yourself in yoga class, on your back, so relaxed you feel like you're floating. That's no metaphor at BayCreek Paddling Center's stand-up paddleboard yoga class—at least during end-of-class Savasana. The balancing act begins once anchored in a secluded spot on Irondequoit Creek, a tranquil waterway that feeds Irondequoit Bay before flowing into Lake Ontario. On ancient remnants of the Genesee River, rerouted long ago by retreating glaciers, it's easy to ignore nearby traffic sounds and tune into serene surroundings: towering cattails, water lilies, swans, ducks resting on one leg (their version of tree pose?). Ten minutes are devoted to "playtime," an invitation to experiment with preferred movements according to comfort level and risk tolerance. The boost to your spirit alone is worth the $30 cost.

1099 Empire Blvd., 585-288-2830
www.baycreek.com

ESCAPE TO A BOTANICAL OASIS
AT LAMBERTON CONSERVATORY

It's easy to be mesmerized by room after room of exotic flowers and foliage in the glass-walled Lamberton Conservatory. But watch where you walk—two species of quail and a free-roaming tortoise have the right of way. Take advantage of the occasional bench to marvel at cascading air plants, flamboyant birds-of-paradise, and other tropical and desert displays. The ever-changing light makes this Highland Park gem perfect for contemplation. The conservatory's motto: "Making visitors horticulturally happy since 1911." It's hard to imagine, but everything here is watered by hand. Not that you could, but don't miss the spectacular staghorn fern in the second room, which also houses an orchid collection. Seasonal exhibits change five times a year. (Holiday poinsettias get their own turn.)

180 Reservoir Ave., 585-753-7270
www.monroecounty.gov/parks-conservatory

STROLL
ON THE NOT-SO-SECRET SIDEWALK

Admire elegantly manicured lawns and water views attached to some of Rochester's most prized real estate. Sauntering along a hidden stretch of sidewalk hugging the Lake Ontario coast, it might feel like you're trespassing, but Rochester's Secret Sidewalk is actually a city-owned right-of-way open to the general public. One property along the third-of-a-mile jaunt offers a bench and handmade sign encouraging visitors to sit down and relax. Listen to waves and seagulls. Look for inspiration in pristine gardens. And remember that this is a residential area, so please be respectful. Though dog-friendly, bikes and skateboards aren't allowed.

TIP
The lakeside Secret Sidewalk is off Beach Avenue, several blocks west of Ontario Beach Park. The easiest way to find the western entryway is by parking on Cloverdale Street. To enter from the east, park on Clematis Street and look for the start of the sidewalk near the flagpole and curving split-rail fence.

COZY UP
ON A SLEIGH RIDE
AT THE HEBERLE STABLES

Hear those sleigh bells jingling as Percheron draft horses pull you on a private ride through Ellison Park. Make it a quiet, romantic excursion (snuggling beneath heavy antique sleigh blankets) or chat with the coachman, dressed true to form in a top hat and long, black wool coat. Be led along Irondequoit Creek, the preglacial route of the Genesee River. Cross over bridges, through groves of pine trees, and past the Lost City of Tryon and Fort Schuyler historical sites. Pet horses and warm up by a bonfire beforehand or afterward. The half-hour Heberle Stables sleigh rides accommodate one to four people. No snow, no problem. The sleigh can be substituted for a carriage instead.

751 Browncroft Blvd., 585-654-9027
www.heberlestables.com

APPRECIATE DIVERSE NEIGHBORHOODS
WITH A HOUSE AND GARDEN TOUR

Offering peeks into private homes since the 1960s, the Landmark Society of Western New York's largest annual fundraiser is one of the oldest house and garden tours in the country. Every year stars a different neighborhood. From monstrous mansions to airy midcentury modern ranch houses—sometimes a mix of both just streets apart—you'll get a history of the neighborhood, details about architectural styles, and a chance to go inside some residences. Historic civic buildings also make an occasional appearance. Tickets are limited for the self-guided walking tours, held on a weekend in June, especially for popular neighborhoods. Allow at least two hours, longer if you like casually strolling through beautiful streetscapes. And be sure to wear comfortable shoes.

Landmark Society of Western New York, 585-546-7029
www.landmarksociety.org/housetour

RUN LIKE HELL
TO RAISE MONEY FOR CHARITY

Tie one on at the annual Halloween-themed "Run Like Hell" 5K race sponsored by Johnny's Irish Pub. Tether yourself to five others (race organizers, who say there's a strategy here, provide the string) and make your way as a six-pack to the finish line. Costumes are encouraged. One recent team dressed up as female historymakers, including Rosie the Riveter and Ruth Bader Ginsberg. You can also run solo in the all-ages race, which winds through Irondequoit neighborhoods, where residents cheer from the sidelines and hand out beers near the finish line. Prizes include $100 pub gift cards for the fastest and most creatively dressed teams. Stick around afterward for free sheet pizza. Proceeds benefit local charities.

Johnny's Irish Pub
1382 Culver Rd., 585-224-0990
www.johnnyslivemusic.com

585-417-5575
www.robinhoodraces.com

SUPPORT A BIRD
ON ITS MIGRATORY ROUTE
AT BRADDOCK BAY

Each spring northwest of Rochester, millions of birds pass through Braddock Bay, on Lake Ontario's southern shore, to rest and refuel before making their next migratory jump. Researchers at the nonprofit, volunteer-run Braddock Bay Bird Observatory study around 10,000 of them annually—measuring and weighing their avian visitors before documenting how they behave during stopovers. Observe the work at a public banding station, once featured on National Public Radio's "Science Friday" program. Help release a bird outfitted with a uniquely numbered band (some will make their way to Central and South America), even listen to a heartbeat. Love the process and want more of it? The observatory is one of only a handful in the United States and Canada that offer structured training for new banders.

10 Braddocks Ave., Hilton, 585-227-3490
www.braddockbaybirdobservatory.wordpress.com

GLIDE ON GLACIAL TERRAIN
AT MENDON PONDS PARK

Rochester is not well known as a ski destination, but it can claim training ground good enough for national-level cross-country ski racers. Classical and skate skiers can cover more than 12 miles of trails at Mendon Ponds Park. Eskers, kames, and land kettles—landforms caused by melting glaciers—create routes of varying terrain and difficulty levels. Maps are posted online and at kiosks. The 10K Esker Loop course is best on classic skis, and the mostly flat Quaker Pond Loop is popular with beginners. Trails stay well-maintained thanks to groomers from the Rochester XC Ski Foundation. Easily visible signage points out trail names, one-way areas, and ski etiquette. With free skiing and free parking, what's there to lose? (Well, maybe your balance.)

95 Douglas Rd., Mendon
www.monroecounty.gov/parks-mendonponds

TIP

There are many starting points for cross-country skiing at Mendon Ponds Park. The most popular place to park for the 10K Esker Loop trail is on Canfield Road just east of the Douglas Road intersection. The Lookout lot is best for the Quaker Pond Loop trail.

AMBLE
(LIKE THE MULES ONCE DID)
ALONG THE ERIE CANAL

Of course, you won't be tied to a rope and forced to pull barges. Instead, meander with ease along the Erie Canal towpath, an east-west route dating back to 1822. Choose any one of our region's canal-side villages for a picturesque walk. The Village of Brockport to the west is known for its Victorian ambience. Heading east from there are the villages of Spencerport, Pittsford, Fairport, and the hamlet of Bushnell's Basin. After clocking enough steps (does "15 miles on the Erie Canal" ring a bell?), poke around local shops and restaurants. Each community has at least one ice cream shop and a brewery. Some have museums; all have historical markers.

TIP

When in the Village of Fairport, walk across the landmark Lift Bridge. It's the only lift bridge in the world in which, to compensate for an incline, no two angles are the same—an engineering marvel captured in a *Ripley's Believe It or Not!* daily cartoon in September 2022.

Village of Brockport
www.brockportny.org

Village of Spencerport
www.vil.spencerport.ny.us/vil

Village of Pittsford
www.villageofpittsford.com

Village of Fairport
www.village.fairport.ny.us

Bushnell's Basin
www.facebook.com/people/Bushnells-Basin-
Perfectly-Perinton/100064521708763

PADDLE THE WATERS OF A HISTORIC RIVER
WITH GENESEE WATERWAYS CENTER

The north-flowing Genesee River is where wildlife and history meet. From a kayak or canoe, catch sight of hawks, blue herons, painted turtles, maybe even an eagle along the river—called "pleasant banks" by the Iroquois in the 18th century. Expect your experience to be pleasant, with beautiful scenery in a serene setting. On the few days when Letchworth State Park to the south opens up the dam in the Genesee River Gorge, paddlers go with the flow a bit faster. It's a 20- to 30-minute paddle downtown, downriver. (Abundant signage ensures you turn around before the High Falls waterfall.) The other direction points toward the Erie Canal and up Red Creek. Rentals from Genesee Waterways Center are good for three- to six-hour stints.

149 Elmwood Ave., 585-328-3960

www.geneseewaterways.org

OTHER FOLKS THAT CAN HELP YOU HIT THE WATER

BayCreek Paddling Center
1099 Empire Blvd., Penfield, 585-288-2830
www.baycreek.com

Lock 32 Paddling Center
2797 Clover St., Pittsford, 585-586-4330
www.lock32.com

Erie Canal Boat Company
7 Liftbridge Lane West, Village of Fairport,
585-748-2628
www.eriecanalboatcompany.com

Rochester Accessible Adventures
585-491-6011
www.rochesteraccessibleadventures.org

UNWIND
IN SCENIC WOODLAND
AT CORBETT'S GLEN NATURE PARK

Seek respite at this 52-acre getaway minutes from downtown. Carved by glaciers and home to a variety of habitats, Corbett's Glen Nature Park is most known for two miles of wide, well-marked trails and three diminutive cascades, including Postcard Falls. Pass through the historic Corbett's Glen Tunnel, just past a privately owned house—once belonging to Patrick Corbett, known as the Celery King—to find a binder dangling from a kiosk. Open it. Tons of vintage photos—including the tunnel as it looked in 1900—sweep you back to a time when picnickers wore petticoats. (President Abraham Lincoln's funeral train passed on railroad tracks above the tunnel in 1865.) No bathrooms, no wading in Allen's Creek (officially speaking), and limited parking.

www.corbettsglen.org

TIP

There are two ways to enter Corbett's Glen Nature Park. Just off Interstate 490 and near Route 441, park at the top of Glen Road and walk through the Corbett's Glen Tunnel (for quickest access to the kiosk). Or use an eight-car parking lot located off Penfield Road, across from Forest Hill Road.

HIKE THE "GRAND CANYON OF THE EAST"
AT LETCHWORTH STATE PARK

With a 17-mile glacier-carved gorge, three major waterfalls, and cliffs as high as 600 feet, Letchworth State Park comes by its moniker honestly. *USA Today* readers named it the country's best state park in 2015. Lots of routes to choose from, with 66 miles of hiking trails. The moderate, seven-mile Gorge Trail, following the west side of the Genesee River, is most popular for the nearly nonstop, breathtaking views. Marketed as New York's most versatile park, Letchworth includes the Autism Nature Trail, a one-mile loop with a series of eight sensory stations and a first for state parks nationwide. About 50 minutes down the road from Rochester, but visiting is unquestionably worth the trip.

1 Letchworth State Park, Castile, 585-493-3600
www.parks.ny.gov/parks/letchworth

TIP
Gain access to Letchworth State Park with a day-use fee or Empire Pass Card. Admission is free between November and mid-May, or any time of year if entering before 9 a.m. or after 5 p.m.

BUST OUT YOUR BICYCLE
AFTER A LONG WINTER

There's a reason *Bicycling* magazine once named Rochester one of the top bike-friendly cities in the United States. Criteria for the designation included catering to different kinds of riders, and we have it all—from recreational, easy rides on flat ground to challenging off-road and mountain-biking trails. (The magazine also praised our "smart, savvy bike shops.") Our metro area has over 230 miles of multiuse trails and 60 on-street lane miles, and more are being added every year. For some of the most attractive routes in New York State, strap on a helmet as soon as spring has sprung.

Genesee Riverway Trail
Scenic, flat, 24 miles long, and runs through the heart of Rochester along the Genesee River.
www.cityofrochester.gov/grt

Erie Canalway Trail
Views of Erie Canal boats, bridges, and locks while cycling on a historic route.
www.ptny.org/cycle-the-erie-canal/trail-map

Auburn Trail
Created from a former railroad corridor, a mostly tree-lined route in rural countryside.
www.victorhikingtrails.org/map/trails/auburn.php

Dryer Road Park
Multiuse trail system for cyclists of all levels.
www.mygroc.com/trails/dryer-road-park

Turning Point Park
Multiuse trail includes a boardwalk over the Genesee River and regular sightings of herons, swans, and other wildlife.
www.cityofrochester.gov/turningpoint

Tryon Park
Predominantly for expert cyclists—with log bridges, jumps, and obstacles in rugged and natural terrain.
www.mygroc.com/trails/tryon-park

George Eastman Museum
Photo courtesy Michael DeMaria

CULTURE
AND HISTORY

FIND THE FAMOUS
AT MOUNT HOPE CEMETERY

Susan B. Anthony, Frederick Douglass, and Lillian Wald are among notable figures buried at the 196-acre Mount Hope Cemetery, the nation's first municipal Victorian cemetery. Find them on your own with a map available on the main office door, or take a guided walking tour. A magnificent display of monuments, sculptures, and mausoleums blanket the dramatic, undulating landscape formed by glaciers (and beloved by exercise buffs). The historic north end is like an architectural museum, with a Victorian Gothic gatehouse, Moorish gazebo, Florentine cast-iron fountain, and Gothic Revival-style stone chapel. Photographers and bird watchers are drawn to the more than 120 tree species (most with QR codes for scanning interesting facts). On the National Register of Historic Places, this peaceful memorial park is a treasure year-round.

791 Mount Hope Ave.

www.fomh.org

TIP

Between May and October, the nonprofit Friends of Mount Hope Cemetery leads theme tours (with titles such as "Mourning Rituals in 19th Century America" and "Mischief, Murder, and Mayhem") every Saturday, general tours on Sundays, and twilight tours on Thursday evenings. All 60- to 90-minute tours cost $12 unless otherwise specified.

EXPOSE YOURSELF TO THE HISTORY OF FILM
AT GEORGE EASTMAN MUSEUM

Let this sink in: we wouldn't have selfies without hometown hero and Eastman Kodak founder George Eastman. Learn more about the pioneer of popular photography and motion picture film at the George Eastman Museum—both the world's oldest photography museum and site of the National Historic Landmark mansion the entrepreneur and philanthropist lived in from 1905 to 1932. The museum houses unparalleled collections, including one of the world's largest collections of daguerreotypes. Step into a room-size camera obscura for a unique view of the West Garden. Children can explore in a hands-on Discovery Room. Head to Eastman's majestic conservatory on the first Sunday of the month to hear a recital on an Aeolian pipe organ, the largest residential organ in the country. Free parking.

900 East Ave., 585-327-4800

www.eastman.org

TIP

Docent and self-guided tours of contemporary and historic photography exhibition galleries, George Eastman's mansion, and gardens are offered to any visitor. Members, however, get special access to behind-the-scenes events and other perks.

GET A CRASH COURSE IN HISTORY
AT AN ARCHITECTURE FOR LUNCH TOUR

Interested in a brief lunchtime history lesson? Tyler Lucero's your man. A former Landmark Society of Western New York staffer, he leads free, 20-minute walking presentations on the history and architecture of downtown Rochester neighborhoods. Keep up with him because there's a lot to cover. "The landscape is a text just like a will or census tract—it tells stories about the past," Tyler says. A tour of the East End and historic Grove Place neighborhood passes some of the oldest locust trees in the city and the workshop once owned by George Selden, who invented the internal combustion engine and sued Henry Ford for patent infringement. (He won, then lost on appeal.) Usually on Wednesdays in the summer, but check with the Landmark Society.

585-546-7029
www.landmarksociety.org

FOLLOW IN THE FOOTSTEPS
OF FREDERICK DOUGLASS

The Frederick Douglass National Historic Site may be in the nation's capital, but Rochester is where the escaped slave-turned-internationally-renowned orator did some of the most important work of his career. A self-guided tour of more than a dozen locations around Rochester spotlights stops integral to the life and legacy of the most photographed man of the 19th century. You'll see where Douglass published the abolitionist newspaper, the *North Star*, and where he delivered his famous "What to the Slave Is the Fourth of July?" speech. Douglass lived here longer than anywhere else, from 1847 to 1872. The landscape may have changed since then (the site of his family farm is now an elementary school) but the social reformer's message is just as resonant.

www.douglasstour.com/tour

STAND AT THE SITE OF A FAMED ARREST
AT SUSAN B. ANTHONY'S HOUSE

Home for 40 years to one of the world's greatest revolutionaries, the National Susan B. Anthony Museum & House celebrates one of the most famous faces of the women's suffrage movement. Walk along the same slate sidewalk the political force once strolled. Learn about her close relationships with abolitionists Elizabeth Cady Stanton and Frederick Douglass. Ponder a moment in the parlor, where Anthony was arrested for voting illegally in the 1872 presidential election—48 years before the ratification of the 19th Amendment, which gave women the right to vote. This unassuming National Historic Landmark is chock full of artifacts and research materials documenting the feminist's lifelong struggle for human rights. Take a docent-led tour for inspiring behind-the-scenes stories. Closed on Mondays.

17 Madison St., 585-235-6124

TIP

Around the corner is Susan B. Anthony Square Park, where Rochester sculptor Pepsy Kettavong's bronze sculpture titled "Let's Have Tea" depicts Anthony and Douglass having a conversation. About three blocks away, at 439 W. Main St., is the "1872 Monument," a bronze locked ballot box sculpture (also by Kettavong) depicting the site where Anthony cast her illegal ballot for Ulysses S. Grant in his reelection bid. If all this history makes you hungry, stop into the 1872 Cafe, at 431 W. Main St., for a snack.

EXPAND YOUR DEFINITION OF ART
AT ARTISANWORKS

The art world is a hotbed of nonconformity, and ARTISANworks is like its mothership. Sensory overload alert: unlike galleries with stark walls, founder Louis Perticone's quirky, cluttered collection of paintings, photography, taxidermy, and more—every piece of it for sale or lease—fills almost every inch of a 100,000-square-foot renovated factory. Wandering the sprawling layout can take hours, especially if you explore its nooks and crannies, where you'll find a 1981 DMC DeLorean, a $100,000 Lionel train collection, and several theme rooms, including a re-creation of Rick's American Café from the movie *Casablanca*. General admission hours are Friday through Sunday. Weekend tours, included with your ticket, usually are offered by Perticone himself, who likes to say, "The backstories are often more interesting than the pieces themselves."

565 Blossom Rd., Suite L, 585-288-7170
www.artisanworks.net

REFLECT ON 5,000 YEARS OF CREATIVE EXPRESSION
AT MEMORIAL ART GALLERY

The University of Rochester's Memorial Art Gallery boasts over 13,000 pieces in its collection—from an Egyptian mummy to work from contemporary art star Rashid Johnson. Permanent collection faves include paintings by Maxfield Parrish, Georgia O'Keeffe, Jacob Lawrence, and Claude Monet, as well as world-class artists from our own backyard: American modernist metal sculptor Albert Paley and Wendell Castle, father of the American art furniture movement, whose cast-iron Unicorn Family sculpture helps anchor the gallery's outdoor Centennial Sculpture Park. Pia Camil's "Lover's Rainbow"—a monumental structure made of painted stainless steel rebar—is one of the park's newest additions. There's no charge to languish at tables in the front atrium, beneath the largest skylight in Rochester and surrounded by Alexander Calder and Henry Moore sculptures.

500 University Ave., 585-276-8900
www.mag.rochester.edu

TIP

On Sundays at 1:30 and 3 p.m., Eastman School of Music students give 25-minute performances, included with admission, on the only full-size, antique Italian baroque organ in North America.

WALK ON SACRED GROUND
AT GANONDAGAN STATE HISTORIC SITE

Learn about Native American history in a way no classroom can match. Ganondagan is a National Historic Landmark and the only original, 17th-century Seneca townsite of its kind in the United States. More than 4,000 people once peacefully lived here, until the town's destruction in 1687. From May to October, tour a full-size, fully furnished bark longhouse—a replica of the 150 that once stood on these grounds. Explore an extensive gallery of Seneca history, culture, and art at the Seneca Art & Culture Center. Numerous interpretive signs aid on self-guided tree identification and medicine walk hikes. Discover the multitude of ways this indigenous culture influenced our modern understanding of equality, democracy, women's rights, ecology, and natural foods.

7000 County Rd. 41, Victor, 585-924-5848
www.ganondagan.org

DISCOVER AN EMERGING ARTIST
AT ROCHESTER CONTEMPORARY ART CENTER

What do Thích Nhất Hạnh, Philip Glass, and Louise Slaughter have in common? They've all contributed to Rochester Contemporary Art Center's annual 6x6 exhibition, which brings together roughly 6,000 original artworks—all measuring six inches square—from people of all ages and backgrounds. The works pour in from at least 40 countries and every US state for the summer installation. Some are whimsical, some seriously address social and political issues, some come from the minds of grade-schoolers. All are exhibited anonymously; buy one for $20 to reveal the artist's name. Proceeds support the center, where at other times of the year gallery shows by both renowned and emerging artists rotate every two months.

137 East Ave., 585-461-2222
www.rochestercontemporary.org

MOVE THROUGH THREE TIME PERIODS
AT GENESEE COUNTRY VILLAGE & MUSEUM

Spanning from 1795 to 1900, the Genesee Country Village & Museum is the country's third-largest working, 19th-century living history museum. About 20 miles from Rochester, the museum boasts the largest and most comprehensive collection of historic buildings in New York State. Talk with knowledgeable, costumed interpreters as they cook over hearths, nurture heirloom gardens, and tend livestock. Sample authentic "receipts" (called recipes today) in homes throughout the village. Watch live pottery and blacksmith demonstrations. Roll a hoop with a stick on the village square. The museum's regular season is May through October, but seasonal events are offered in the off-season (check out the Maple Sugar Festival in March). Grab a strawberry-rhubarb hand pie at the D. B. Munger Confectionery on your way out.

1410 Flint Hill Rd., Mumford, 585-538-6822
www.gcv.org

DEEPEN YOUR PERCEPTION
AT VISUAL STUDIES WORKSHOP

For art lovers who bend toward the avant-garde, the VSW Salon at Visual Studies Workshop does not disappoint. In an informal, intimate space at this internationally recognized center for media studies, the bimonthly series is best approached with an open mind. Of the typical variety: a filmmaker using 16mm projectors at controlled speeds to loop films until they melt, or two video game glitch artists overlaying interrupted attempts at play with poetry about complicated father-son relationships. Aside from artist talks and other events, the series lets regional community groups curate film screenings with the workshop's collection of over 10,000 film and video titles. Arrive early to talk with workshop artists-in-residence. Free on the second and fourth Thursday of the month; suggested donations are $5 to $10.

31 Prince St., 585-442-8676

www.vsw.org

SEE THE CITY'S SOUL
THROUGH WALL\THERAPY'S OUTDOOR MURAL ART

The art is colorful, visually arresting, and in some cases several stories high. Rochester's WALL\THERAPY mural project, an experiment in using public art to transform urban spaces, is recognized worldwide. People in more than 104 countries have visited its website to learn why artists from Italy, Sweden, Germany, Brazil, and beyond have traveled here to paint murals that reflect the world around them. Local artists have offered their own contributions to the portraiture, abstract expression, typography, and other art forms displayed in full view throughout the city. National Public Radio profiled the open-air art gallery, now with more than 135 installations, in 2014. An early progenitor of the modern mural festival, the project even has merch.

www.wall-therapy.com
www.visitrochester.com/blog/post/top-spots-public-art-rochester

ADMIRE
THE BEST IN CLAY
AT THE FLOWER CITY ARTS CENTER

The Flower City Pottery Invitational is a highly curated national event in the ceramics world—a weekend dedicated to spotlighting one of the oldest human inventions. Some 20 emerging and established makers from around the United States exhibit their take on the extremely versatile material. From fine porcelain to functional earthenware, from contemporary designs to rustic tableware, all items are for sale and vastly distinct. The event is held in October at the Flower City Arts Center, and includes demonstrations (perhaps witness the creation of a teapot) and lectures (ever wonder about the influence of ancient bisque molds?). All very apropos in a region where pottery-making communities date back to the 18th century and were influential in the Arts & Crafts movement. Free admission; a Friday-night reception costs $35.

713 Monroe Ave., 585-244-1730
www.flowercityarts.org

TOWER
ABOVE THE LAKEFRONT
AT CHARLOTTE–GENESEE LIGHTHOUSE

What's the fun of going to a lighthouse if you don't climb to the tippy-top? At the Charlotte–Genesee Lighthouse, that requires ascending a 42-step circular staircase and an 11-rung ladder. The reward is a bird's-eye view of Lake Ontario and the Charlotte Pier, Genesee River, and Port of Rochester. First built in 1822, the 55-foot-high stone structure is the oldest surviving lighthouse on Lake Ontario's southern shore, which stretches from Lake Erie to the St. Lawrence River. A restoration in 2014 incorporated a replica of the original lighthouse lens once run on whale oil and now on 12 LED lights, making the lighthouse visible from 12 miles away on a clear day. Tours also include the Keeper's House, now a museum and gift shop.

70 Lighthouse St., 585-621-6179
www.geneseelighthouse.org

Charlotte–Genesee Lighthouse
Photo courtesy Michael DeMaria

HANDLE HISTORY
AT THE UNIVERSITY OF ROCHESTER

The University of Rochester's Department of Rare Books, Special Collections, and Preservation sounds elite but is open to all. Thanks to donations over decades, it holds the largest collection of historical materials about Rochester. There's a formal procedure for gaining access to those materials—and for handling them—but be eager to sign up. We're talking handwritten letters by Susan B. Anthony and Frederick Douglass. And photographs, public-relations materials, and international records from Eastman Kodak Company. The department also owns medieval manuscripts and the largest collection of HIV/AIDS education posters in the world. Religion, horticulture, science, women's and LGBTQI history—the list goes on. A visit to this free, nonlending library is priceless in more ways than one.

755 Library Rd., 585-275-4477
www.library.rochester.edu/rbscp

TIP

You'll need to pay to park in the University of Rochester's Library Lot. The route to the Department of Rare Books, Special Collections, and Preservation is long and winding, but equipped with a full paragraph of detailed directions provided by staff beforehand, the journey should be stress-free.

LEARN HOW TRAVEL EVOLVED
AT THE NEW YORK MUSEUM OF TRANSPORTATION

Travel through time at the New York Museum of Transportation, home to vehicles that trace the evolution of transit from horse-drawn buggies to automobiles. (Local residents of a certain age will appreciate the classic Midtown Plaza monorail car.) Ring the bell on a steam locomotive. Climb aboard an exquisitely restored trolley with vintage brass hardware you'd never find at Home Depot. See a bona fide handcar and tons of ephemera left over from the abandoned Rochester Subway. Located 20 minutes south of Rochester, the museum also exhibits a gargantuan model railroad with three trains running simultaneously. Open Sundays only, mid-May through October, the museum features scenic, two-mile round-trip trolley rides.

6393 E. River Rd., Rush, 585-533-1113

www.nymtmuseum.org

TIP

Two miles down the road, in a restored 1909 Erie Railroad depot, is the Rochester & Genesee Valley Railroad Museum. The depot holds the largest collection of historic trains and operating vintage diesel locomotives in New York State, though not all are on display. Train rides offered during special events only.

282 Rush Scottsville Rd., Rush, 585-533-1431
www.rgvrrm.org

CONTEMPLATE COMMUNICATION
AT THE CARY GRAPHIC ARTS COLLECTION

Next to the Gutenberg Bible, the Kelmscott Chaucer is considered to be the most outstanding typographic achievement of all time—and the press used by William Morris to print it is right here in Rochester. The Cary Graphic Arts Collection at Rochester Institute of Technology is one of the world's premier libraries and research centers on graphic communication history and practices, open to the public for lectures, workshops, classes, and exhibitions. Look at a clay tablet from 2100 BCE (the collection's earliest artifact). Sit at a Renaissance bookwheel. Wade through the archive of original calligraphy, design work, posters, books, and letters belonging to the late Hermann Zapf, who created Optima, Palatino, and some 200 other typefaces. Appointments accepted after an extensive renovation is completed in fall 2023.

90 Lomb Memorial Dr., 585-475-3961
www.rit.edu/carycollection

RAISE A GLASS
TO SPIRITUALISM
AT THE SPIRIT ROOM

A classroom can be anywhere, so when it comes to learning about how Rochester birthed one of the greatest religious movements of the 19th century, it may as well be in a bar. At the Spirit Room, the 11-page drink menu is a miniature chapbook summarizing the history behind each cocktail name—all commemorating the rise and fall of Spiritualism, ignited by three local sisters who shot to fame with public séances. (Their picture is by a front-door altar.) Order "The Fox Sisters" for a delicate, Victorian-era blend of bourbon, Earl Grey tea, lavender syrup, lemon, and egg white. Not all books have happy endings. True to history, this one reports how Leah, Maggie, and Kate Fox fell from grace after confessing their paranormal experiences were a hoax.

139 State St., 585-397-7595

www.spiritroomroc.com

TIP

Get into the spirit of the place with a front-alcove tarot reading for $10 (Thursdays through Saturdays). Or, when owner Jacob Rakovan is working, allow him to consult the tarot and craft a cocktail based on the recommendations he receives.

CLIMB ABOARD THE
SAM PATCH PACKET BOAT
ON THE LEGENDARY ERIE CANAL

Gigantic steel doors open to let 2.8 million gallons of water fill Lock 32 on the Erie Canal, lifting water levels 25 feet in minutes—and you're on a boat in the middle of it all. This experience comes courtesy of the *Sam Patch*, a replica packet boat named after the first famous American daredevil (who perished after jumping off Rochester's High Falls). A 90-minute cruise offers a rare perspective on the man-made waterway—nicknamed "The Eighth Wonder of the World" and once responsible for making Rochester one of the country's premier commercial and financial centers. Look for herons and eagles while hearing about what went into digging this National Historic Landmark. Before disembarking, join in a rendition of the popular "Low Bridge, Everybody Down" song. Bathroom on board.

12 Schoen Place, Pittsford, 585-662-5748
www.sampatch.org

TIP

If you prefer to tour the Erie Canal on a larger boat, schedule a ride on the *Colonial Belle*. Standard cruises last between two and three hours, depending on the tour you choose. Murder Mystery Dinner Cruises and other themed events are offered.

400 Packett's Landing, Village of Fairport
585-223-9470
www.colonialbelle.com

DOTE ON THE HOMES
IN ROCHESTER'S OLDEST
NEIGHBORHOOD

Once called Rochesterville, the Corn Hill neighborhood is flush with history. This is where city founder Colonel Nathaniel Rochester and other wealthy settlers lived, leading to the nicknames "Ruffled Shirt Ward" and "Silk Stocking District." It was here that the city's first Black church, the African Methodist Episcopal Zion Church, doubled as a stop on the Underground Railroad and the place where Frederick Douglass published his abolitionist newspaper, the *North Star*. Walk along well-preserved streets to admire the architectural details on Victorian homes that, on the brink of extinction in the 1960s, became one of the country's earliest urban restoration success stories. For two days in August, tens of thousands attend the Corn Hill Arts Festival, a celebration of original art and music since 1969.

Begin your walk at a small pocket park.
281 S. Plymouth Ave., 585-262-3142
www.cornhill.org

TIP

The Clarissa Street of yesteryear is mostly unrecognizable now. Most buildings were demolished as a result of urban renewal policies and downtown construction. But in its heyday, its jazz clubs attracted big-name musicians who played for elbow-to-elbow crowds, and it was a thriving corridor of Black-owned businesses. The Clarissa Street Reunion, an annual music-filled festival in August, pays tribute to what once was referred to as "Rochester's Broadway."

Peppermint
Photo courtesy Tanvi Asher

SHOPPING
AND FASHION

REVEL IN THE VESTIGES OF ROCK ROYALTY
AT HOUSE OF GUITARS

It doesn't matter whether you're in the market for a guitar. Pop over to the part-retail, part-museum House of Guitars to ogle instruments autographed by rock legends, John Lennon's military jacket, and, if timed right, a famous musician in for an impromptu gig before a show. Get lost in a multilevel maze of rooms showcasing new, used, rare, and vintage guitars. Walls hold thousands of old pictures and autographs—one flaunts hundreds of signatures from music industry titans. The Ramones even appeared in a House of Guitars commercial. Two brothers who started the business in 1964 out of the basement of their mother's home still work hard to create a vibe that has earned House of Guitars its motto: "The store that ate your brain."

645 Titus Ave., 585-544-3500
www.houseofguitars.com

VISIT THE MECCA OF GROCERY STORES
AT WEGMANS

Tens of thousands of Wegmans grocery store fans show up for grand openings, the most devout devotees in T-shirts labeling them as Wegmaniacs. But only Rochesterians can claim the 109-store chain as their own since 1916. The original location stands no longer, but the grocer's longest-running store in East Rochester retains the upswept roofline and other midcentury details from 1958. After Cher visited the 133,000-square-foot Wegmans in Pittsford, she wanted one built in California. Why all the fuss? A gigantic selection of international foods, cheese, and premade entrées and sides; ultrafresh produce (some from local growers); and flowers from the company's organic farm in the Finger Lakes—all reminiscent of a European open-air market.

851 Fairport Rd., East Rochester, 585-586-8340
3195 Monroe Ave., Pittsford, 585-586-6680

For more local locations:
www.wegmans.com

GLOBE-TROT WITHOUT A PASSPORT
AT BEERS OF THE WORLD

Resembling a superstore with bright lights and lengthy aisles, Beers of the World is a libation lover's paradise. Find imported and domestic brews from 29 states and 57 countries, including hard-to-get brews from Israel, Kenya, and Lithuania. Home of the single-bottle sale, the store encourages trying a variety of beers (gluten-free and nonalcoholic among them) without committing to a particular label; cardboard six-pack holders are at the entrance for customizing mix-and-match samplers. Head over on a weekend and you might stumble across a tasting. Co-owner Susan Clapper grew up in the store, founded by her father, who was the first to bring the Belgian blond beer La Chouffe to the US. (That's for sale here, too.)

2599 E. Henrietta Rd., 585-334-0034
www.mybeersoftheworld.com

HUNT FOR DEEP CUTS
AT RECORD ARCHIVE

Feast your eyes—and ears—on the largest vinyl record collection in the Northeast. An astounding 250,000 LPs cram Record Archive, a funky auditory playground packed with every form of new and used prerecorded media. Along a wall near the entrance, beneath a ceiling lined with dangling banana-seated bikes, find $5 mystery bags of music (choose from cassettes and CDs; gamble on the artists). Just as entertaining are the toys, a hodgepodge of novelty trinkets and retro faves. If you like the smell of the day's incense, you can buy that, too. Three listening stations allow customers to try before they buy—one for CDs, two for records. (You're in the Record Archive, after all.) In business since 1975, this store is 13,000 square feet of fun.

33⅓ Rockwood St., 585-244-1210
www.recordarchive.com

TIP

The Backroom Lounge serves beer and wine daily from noon to close, with live tunes on Wednesday nights and an equally eclectic atmosphere—area rugs, a leopard-print couch, and an original red velvet pod chair from *The Dating Game*.

DRESS LIKE AN A-LISTER
AT ROCHESTER TAILORED CLOTHING FACTORY STORE

They were good enough for the Rat Pack and John F. Kennedy. George Eastman preferred them. Hickey Freeman suits have had a long-standing reputation since the luxury menswear clothier was founded in Rochester in 1899. Ready-to-wear and made-to-measure suits—some partially handmade—come in patterns with depth, and are mostly constructed with fabrics from Italy and the United Kingdom. Most suits in the Rochester store were made in Rochester, in the original factory on North Clinton Avenue. Prices start at $500, at least 40% off retail prices. Expect highly personalized service, making it easy to understand why the retailer was widely known back in the day as the "Temple of Fine Tailoring."

The corner of East Broad and South Union streets

SEARCH OUT ON-TREND FASHIONS
AT PEPPERMINT

Find feminine, colorful, fashion-forward pieces in eye-catching patterns at Peppermint. Any clothing or accessory that has the boutique's name on the label was conceptualized and designed by owner Tanvi Asher, who launched her brand in 2011 after earning a master's degree in industrial design from Rochester Institute of Technology. Located in the historic Culver Road Armory, the store is named after the peppermint oil Asher's fashion-savvy grandmother used to wear. Manufactured mostly in Los Angeles, Peppermint's dresses, skirts, tops, knits, and outerwear are carried in stores around the country. European and fair-trade designers, along with hard-to-find labels, also share rack space downstairs. Head upstairs for a wide array of tasteful Rochester-themed merchandise.

145 Culver Rd., 585-532-8132
www.shop-peppermint.com

TIP
Tanvi Asher also owns Salty, a boutique with more affordable and youthful designs, on nearby Park Avenue.

749 Park Ave., 585-520-7009
www.sheissalty.com

JOIN THE HUSTLE AND BUSTLE
AT ROCHESTER PUBLIC MARKET

Crowned "America's Favorite Farmers Market" in 2010, Rochester Public Market has sold fresh fruits and vegetables at low prices since 1905. (This is where Wegmans got its start in 1916 as the Rochester Fruit & Vegetable Company; Bushart Farms has peddled potatoes here for nearly a century.) Mostly outdoors, with an indoor shed selling seafood, meats, cheese, and more. Specialty food purveyors, food stands (Juan and Maria's Empanada Stop has a cult following), and other independent businesses share market grounds. Open three days a week year-round, with fewer vendors on Tuesdays and Thursdays and upwards of 300 on warmer Saturdays. Be patient with parking—with five free parking lots, you'll find a space somewhere. Stores, restaurants, cafés, and craft beverage manufacturers surround the market and line Railroad Street near the market entrance.

280 North Union St., 585-428-6907
www.cityofrochester.gov/publicmarket

ANNUAL EVENTS AT THE ROCHESTER PUBLIC MARKET

Community Garage Sales
Dozens of garage sales in one location.
www.cityofrochester.gov/garagesales

Flower City Days
Annuals, perennials, shrubs, and garden ornamentation in time for spring planting. Cornell Cooperative Extension's master gardeners are available to answer questions.
www.cityofrochester.gov/flowercitydays

Food Truck Rodeos
Creative mobile cuisine with local brews and bands. Last Wednesday evening of the month, April through September.
www.cityofrochester.gov/foodtruckrodeo

Holidays at the Market
A tradition for over 25 years, with trees, decorations, gifts, holiday foods, visits with Santa, and more.
www.cityofrochester.gov/holidaysatmarket

SHOP YOUR CONSCIENCE
AT ONE WORLD GOODS

Spend your money in Rochester and help support an artisan in one of over 50 developing countries. One World Goods makes sure the craftspeople behind the items in this vibrant marketplace get paid a fair wage for their work. Indian jewelry makers, for instance, carve wooden beads from furniture factory scraps before covering them with sari fabric. Root around for all kinds of interesting wares among the olive oils made with ancient farming methods and batiked string bags recycled from Ghanian flour sacks. Thirty years after its humble start, when a small group of women filled their cars with fair-trade goods to sell at local churches and schools, the nonprofit store, run primarily by volunteers, continues to spread awareness about global poverty and economic injustice.

3349 Monroe Ave., 585-387-0070
www.oneworldgoods.org

TIP

One World Goods holds its annual Fair Trade Rug Event in September. The sale features a large selection of high-quality, fairly traded, hand-knotted tribal, Bokhara, and Persian rugs.

ENVY THE RUNWAY
AT FASHION WEEK OF ROCHESTER

Who needs Milan? Fashion Week of Rochester's annual runway shows push the boundaries of innovation and artistry by local designers and boutiques. Every show has a different theme: ready-to-wear, with families, couples, even dogs in coordinating outfits; gritty, urban looks on the edgier side; couture bridal gowns. Students from Rochester Institute of Technology's School for American Crafts are a crowd favorite, fusing technology, art, and design into ultramodern wearable pieces. The high-energy event draws sellout audiences over multiple nights in October, with appearances by international guest designers. It's a party, so take advantage of the bottle and food service. All proceeds after expenses benefit the Center for Youth's shelter and crisis services.

www.fashionweekofrochester.org

RESTORE THE PAST
WITH HISTORIC HOUSEPARTS

The antique toilet one of the Smurfs got flushed down? The light fixture that fell on Liz Lemon's head? Both came from Historic Houseparts, a well-organized slice of architectural salvage heaven (and parts supplier to the stars). The main building, a circa-1890 row house, offers two floors of antique hardware dating back to the late 1700s, as well as reproductions. (The store has a healthy following of door and cabinet hardware collectors.) Two warehouses are out back—one dedicated to doors, the other to stained glass, shutters, porch posts, bathtubs, and other large finds mined from demolitions and renovations, mostly from Western New York. Plumbing materials have a building all their own. Expect to find everything for the house here—including the kitchen sink.

540 South Ave., 585-325-2329
www.historichouseparts.com

UNEARTH TREASURES
AT THE SHOPS ON WEST RIDGE

Third-generation Shops on West Ridge owner Nile Marple likes the number two. The mall of sorts offers over 200,000 items in 200 shops on two floors. Its Dickens Fest, at which vendors dress in Dickensian clothing, is held over two weekends (one in November, one in December). On the first Friday of November, everything is discounted 20 percent. Go on the first Saturday of the month in hopes of finding one of 200 tokens, good for markdowns in varying amounts, spread throughout the store. The selection is a blend of old and new—antiques, furniture, toys, gifts, locally made crafts. Other attractions: a Midway Lounge with nine leather chairs and three TVs (lively during Buffalo Bills games), and an in-house café. Carry-out and car-loading service available.

3200 W. Ridge Rd., 585-368-0670
www.theshopsonwestridge.com

SCOUR THE SHELVES
AT AN INDEPENDENT BOOKSTORE

For a city our size, Rochester hits pay dirt when it comes to the number of independent bookstores around town—and just beyond. Areas of interest include small-press publications, first editions, antiquarian and rare books, hard-to-find fiction, collections on deaf culture, regional titles by local authors, and more. In Brockport, Lift Bridge Book Shop has stocked two floors of new and used books since 1972. Stop in there—or at one of these other nonchain bookstores (not an all-encompassing list, by any means)—to share love for literature and get recommendations for your next must-read.

45 Main St., Brockport, 585-637-2260
www.liftbridgebooks.com

Ampersand Books at Writers & Books
740 University Ave., 585-473-2590, ext. 107
www.ampersandbooks.org

Greenwood Books
123 East Ave., 585-325-2050
www.greenwoodbookstore.com

Small World Books
425 North St., 585-232-6970
www.facebook.com/smallworldbooks

Hipocampo Children's Books
638 South Ave., 585-461-0161
www.hipocampochildrensbooks.com

Book Culture
28 S. Main St., Pittsford, 585-203-1501
www.bookculture.com

Before Your Quiet Eyes
439 Monroe Ave., 585-563-7851
www.facebook.com/profile.
php?id=100064281775634

LIVEN UP MONOTONOUS MEALS
AT STUART'S SPICES

You're welcomed here from the get-go, with a sign that says "Cumin, We're Open." A premier yet low-key destination for lovers of fresh herbs, blends, rubs, and seasonings, Stuart's Spices specializes in small batches ground and blended on site. More than 200 varieties are all-natural, kosher-certified, and without gluten or MSG. Many are made from original recipes. Amp up ribs, pulled pork, chicken, or trout with the award-winning House Hog Rub blended with—are you ready?—salt, paprika, sugar, black pepper, garlic, onion, liquid smoke, ground chili peppers, rice flour, citric acid, ground mustard, and cayenne. No wonder local restaurants and butcher shops have gotten their proprietary spice blends here since 1992. More than 50 free recipes for the taking are just inside the door.

754 S. Clinton Ave., 585-436-9329
www.stuartsspices.com

TIP
Cooks' World has been the go-to source for home gourmets since 1978.
2179 Monroe Ave., 585-271-1789
www.cooksworld.com

SHOW YOUR LOVE FOR THE ROC
AT LITTLE BUTTON CRAFT

Hometown pride is rampant at Little Button Craft. The entire layout is lush with Rochester-themed jewelry, glassware, prints, and other gifts and goods. The Rochester logo (a combined flour-mill gear and a budding flower to salute the city's evolution from the Flour City to the Flower City) is everywhere. But this is no kitschy souvenir shop. All merchandise—knitting yarn, illustration, photography, needle felting, woodwork, and more—is handcrafted by more than 200 artisans living within 100 miles. Inventory is conscientiously curated, which explains the steady wait list for shelf space. If you want to glorify Rochester without getting inked—yes, logo tats are big in these parts—shopping at Little Button Craft is the next best thing.

658 South Ave., 585-698-6874
www.littlebuttoncraft.com

FULFILL YOUR CHOCOLATE FANTASIES
AT STEVER'S CANDIES

Like a kick of cayenne pepper in your dark chocolate buttons? There's a flavor profile to match any mouth at Stever's Candies, where deciding between the brittles, jellies, caramels, nuggets, and creams is no small feat. A candy store since 1946, Stever's is run by second-generation candy maker Kevin Stever, who uses his father's original recipes, and his wife, Leslie, who often hears "My grandmother used to bring me here." Employees ring up a sale every 75 seconds at peak holiday times (so bundle up on cold days for lines that can stretch to the sidewalk). Look for chocolate rabbits in spring, saltwater taffy in summer, sponge candy in autumn, and holiday barks in winter.

623 Park Ave., 585-473-2098
www.steverscandy.com

TIP

In the South Wedge neighborhood, Hedonist Artisan Chocolates makes confections with old-world techniques and carefully sourced ingredients. A portion of proceeds from specialty boxes of chocolate-covered salted caramels help support either the Susan B. Anthony Museum & House or the National Women's Hall of Fame in Seneca Falls.

674 South Ave., 585-461-2815
www.hedonistchocolates.com

ENVISION A NEW LOOK
AT ONE HIP CHIC OPTICAL

The selection of spectacles at One Hip Chic Optical is so different, and draws such a spectacularly loyal customer base, it could be called cult eyewear. Premier trade magazine *Invision* named the shop "America's Finest Optical Retailer" in 2020, with one judge observing, "This is a very specific shop for very specific people." Frames are handpicked from the largest eyewear shows in the world, including Paris, Munich, and Milan. Shop by appointment only—allowing one hour for a thorough conversation about color palettes, personality, and tastes. Prices start at $450. No insurance accepted and no contact lenses. No fan of the status quo, owner and optician Tamra Asmuth says she simply wants her business to be about "thought-provoking and genuine" frames.

1521 Monroe Ave., 585-461-2020
www.onehipchic.com

DIG THE ALT SHOPPING SCENE
ON MONROE AVENUE

Abhor trendy malls? Neighboring stores on Monroe Avenue, Rochester's alternative strip, may soothe your unconventional shopping senses. Hippie haven Aaron's Alley is a counterculture staple. It's home to Grateful Dead apparel, gems and minerals, work by more than 85 local artists, and lots and lots of tie-dye. (The concept for the store started in the summer of 1988 with a beach-roaming vendor cart nicknamed Dyed in Heaven). Two doors down, Archimage, family-owned for 40 years, is a pint-sized department store with both incredibly useful and marvelously frivolous goods to satisfy every passion and persuasion. Looking for fake mustaches and zombie finger monsters? Check. What about potted plants and didgeridoos? Check again. Fair warning for sensitive noses: both stores are bathed in incense.

Aaron's Alley
662 Monroe Ave., 585-244-5044
www.facebook.com/aaronsalleyroc

Archimage
668 Monroe Ave., 585-271-2789
www.archimagestore.com

REVIVE RETRO THREADS
AT THE OP SHOP

Wend your way through the decades at the Op Shop, where what once was old is new again. The collective of more than 30 vendors, all carefully vetted, sells upcycled and handmade clothes—including plus sizes difficult to dig up from decades past—from the 1950s to the early 2000s. With the panache of a well-appointed specialty shop, the store boasts some up-and-coming refashion designers, including one tapped to work on a Hermes collection. Operating under the notion that clothing has no gender, owner Joanna Carroll also is for hire for style coaching and wardrobe consultations. Take note of the grand staircase—you're in a house built in 1901—on your way to the second level.

89 Charlotte St., 585-730-1157
www.theopshoproc.com

BROWSE ECLECTIC COLLECTIONS
AT PARKLEIGH

Often voted best gift store by the *Democrat and Chronicle* and *CITY News*, Parkleigh caters to generations of shopping tastes. (On that note, swoon over the truffles and petits fours in the middle of the store.) The most sought-after collections include greeting cards, Jellycat, Kiehl's, Katie Loxton, Chan Luu jewelry, Blue Q, and Stonewall Kitchen. Thirsty? Sample coffees from regional Keuka Lake Coffee Roasters. A former pharmacy, Parkleigh went retail in 1986 and still offers complimentary gift packaging. Cross the street to its second location if you like artisanal, hand-painted designs—it's home to the largest selection of MacKenzie-Childs merchandise in New York State, outside of the colorful brand's flagship store in Manhattan.

215–235 Park Ave., 800-333-0627
www.parkleigh.com

LEARN HOW TO PAMPER BACKYARD GUESTS
AT THE BIRD HOUSE

Interest in birdwatching spiked worldwide during the pandemic. That may be one reason the Bird House sells 10,000 pounds of its own house-blend seeds per week to veteran and budding ornithologists in Rochester. The store claims to have the biggest selection of wild-bird feeders and houses in Western New York. Discerning shoppers can select from more than 50 types of feeders devoted to the agile hummingbird alone. Free events include annual bird feeder cleanings and classes on attracting bluebirds and orioles. Locally owned for more than 25 years, the nature and gift store employs people who love (with a capital L) to talk about birds. If you've ever wanted to know the difference between a finch and a nuthatch, you've found the place to find out.

3035 Monroe Ave., 585-264-1550
www.thebirdhouseny.com

Rochester Public Market
Photo courtesy Michael DeMaria

SUGGESTED
ITINERARIES

DOWNTOWN

FESTIVALS

• •

FOR THE OUTDOOR ENTHUSIAST

THE NATURAL WORLD

FREE AND SOMETIMES FREE

• •

ERIE CANAL

WORTH THE DRIVE

• •

Sea Breeze
Photo courtesy Michael DeMaria

ACTIVITIES
BY SEASON

SPRING

SUMMER

• •

FALL

WINTER

Mercury and *Wings of Progress*
Photo courtesy Michael DeMaria

INDEX

• •